"IF YOU ARE Cmunion, this is the book. If you are in need of a refresher about the Anglican communion, this is the book. Here we get worship, liturgy, prayer, theology, and history — along with living the Christian life — in a short, accessible book. At all levels, this book commends itself as an introduction to the Anglican faith."

—The Rev. Canon Dr. **Scot McKnight**
Professor of New Testament, Northern Seminary

"ANGLICANISM, ALL THE COOL KIDS are doing it, but what is it precisely? In *Simply Anglican*, Winfield Bevins provides an easy to read explanation of Anglicanism, its history, theology, and liturgy. A recommended read for anyone considering becoming Anglican or who wants to know why so many young people are joining Anglican churches."

—The ev. Dr. **Michael F. Bird**
Academic Dean and Lecturer in Theology,
Ridley College, Melbourne, Australia.

"DR. WINFIELD BEVINS WRITES *Simply Anglican* as an outsider and an insider. That duo perspective gives him a vantage and an independent position to evaluate the unique Anglican identity. His journey into Anglicanism is captivating and invites the reader to get deeper into the book to appreciate the richness of Anglicanism. Though simple, it is thoughtful and graciously orthodox. I would recommend this book to both those who are exploring Anglicanism and those Anglicans who need to refresh themselves with the Anglican tradition as told from a fresh perspective."

—Very Rev. Canon **Sammy Wainaina**
All Saints' Cathedral, Nairobi Kenya

"SIMPLY ANGLICAN is a guide to the Anglican way of being Christian that is both reliable and refreshing. It provides an overview of the history, theology, liturgy and mission of this major worldwide expression of the Church that is highly informative and at the same time delightfully motivating. For anyone wanting to understand Anglicanism, this is a great place to start, but it is unlikely to be the end. The reader will want to know more and, I hope, enter more fully into the Anglican way of following Jesus."

—The Rev. Dr. **Justyn Terry**
VICE PRINCIPAL AND ACADEMIC DEAN, WYCLIFFE HALL, OXFORD

"THIS IS THE GUIDE to Anglicanism that I've been waiting for. Bevins provides a tour of the varied nature of a movement and church that will both introduce the Anglican way to beginners and at the same time provide insights for its seasoned members. Rich in historic detail, *Simply Anglican* takes seriously the 'multidimensional nature of discipleship' provided by the various streams of Anglicanism. This is not a guide detached from the men and women who have shaped the Anglican tradition nor its formative documents, from Cranmer to Wesley to Fresh Expressions, the Prayer Book and the Articles of Religion, all brought to life and shown for their missional drive. Bevins' love for Anglicanism can be seen on every page as he describes in accessible terms the ways in which the rich tradition of English Christianity continues to point believers to Christ. I highly recommend *Simply Anglican*!"

—**Ryan Nicholas Danker**
ASSOCIATE PROFESSOR OF THE HISTORY OF CHRISTIANITY AND METHODIST STUDIES, WESLEY THEOLOGICAL SEMINARY AND AUTHOR OF *WESLEY AND THE ANGLICANS*

"MY COLLEAGUE, Winfield Bevins, has written an introduction to Anglicanism that is fresh, easy to grasp and inspired by love for God and a missional heart for one's neighbor. If you are exploring the intersection of liturgy, sacrament and mission, I highly recommend *Simply Anglican*."

—The Rt. Rev. Dr. **Todd Hunter**
BISHOP OF THE DIOCESE OF CHURCHES FOR THE SAKE OF OTHERS, AUTHOR OF *THE ACCIDENTAL ANGLICAN*

"WHEN I DECIDED to embrace the Anglican Tradition, I knew I was taking a big step; that I'd be swimming in deep waters. What I needed was a guide, someone to help me navigate the waters of the Anglican Communion. As the 'new guy,' I needed someone who knew what I was experiencing. I needed someone to tell me, amid uncertainty and a flood of emotions, that I was right where God wanted me to be. I needed someone who spoke the language, who had the time, and, more importantly, the patience, to walk me through history, introduce me to theology, explain the liturgy, and answer my burning questions. Who I needed was Winfield Bevins and *Simply Anglican*."

—The Rev. Canon **Lawrence McElrath**
DIRECTOR OF THE ANGLICAN MULTIETHNIC NETWORK

"I MEET REGULARLY with people who are interested in learning more about Anglicanism but unsure where to start. I'm very pleased that I can now direct them to *Simply Anglican*. It's a trustworthy first-step resource with plenty of direction given for further study. I'm grateful to Winfield Bevins and Anglican Compass for offering such a concise and readable introduction to the Anglican tradition."

—The Rev. Canon Dr. **Emily McGowin**
ASSISTANT PROFESSOR OF THEOLOGY, WHEATON COLLEGE

"THIS IS A BOOK I've been waiting for! I've come to appreciate Anglicanism as a steward of the treasury of early Christian faith and practice. While many are discovering this for themselves, others long to know where to start. Bevins gives a warm, concise, and accessible outline of Anglican history, faith, and worship. But this is much more than an introduction; it is an invitation into a beautiful faith."

—The Rev. Dr. **Glenn Packiam**
ASSOCIATE SENIOR PASTOR, NEW LIFE CHURCH,
AUTHOR, *BLESSED BROKEN GIVEN*

"DR. WINFIELD'S BOOK on Anglicanism is a greatly needed resource for all Christians, but especially new and would-be Anglicans. This easy to understand account of the Anglican way can help shape our new movement. The structure of the book is very, shall we say, Anglican as well. It anchors the faith tradition in the past; the history of our faith. Then it deepens the faith through personal and corporate habits and practices; the life of a believer. And then the book calls us to have a missionary role in the world. That is the essence of Anglicanism itself: Ancient. Authentic. Missional."

—The Rev. Canon **David Roseberry**
Founding Rector, Christ Church Plano

"IN *SIMPLY ANGLICAN*, Winfield Bevins has delivered to us a delightful and eminently readable introduction to Anglicanism. He skillfully guides his readers through the landscape of the Anglican tradition, pausing to glory in its beauties while not losing sight of his destination. I especially appreciate his inclusion of recommended resources and discussion questions for group study, which will be of great benefit to those preparing for Anglican confirmation or reception. Highly recommended!"

—**Joel Scandrett**,
Assistant Professor of Theology,
Trinity School for Ministry

"IN A VERY READABLE introduction, Winfield Bevins lays out the basics of Anglicanism. Covering the basics of Anglican history, theology, and practice, Bevins also emphasizes the mission of the church through the growing global Anglican communion. This book is especially meaningful for those, like the author, who have journeyed to the Anglican church from another church tradition."

—**Edward L. Smither**
Dean, Professor of Intercultural Studies and PhD Program Director, Columbia International University

"IN AN ERA when it has become increasingly difficult to discern what it means to be an Anglican, Winfield Bevins offers us an essential text to communicate our common heritage in his winsome manner. Those new to Anglicanism and those who have been here for decades will find a refreshing and robust book which will be required reading for years to come."

—The Rev. **Porter C. Taylor**
RECTOR, ST. DAVID'S BY THE SEA EPISCOPAL CHURCH
EDITOR OF *WE GIVE OUR THANKS UNTO THEE: ESSAYS IN MEMORY OF FR. ALEXANDER SCHMEMANN*

SIMPLY ANGLICAN

AN ANCIENT FAITH FOR TODAY'S WORLD

WINFIELD BEVINS

SIMPLY ANGLICAN:
An Ancient Faith for Today's World
Copyright 2020 by Winfield Bevins

All rights reserved. No part of this publication may be reproduced, stored in a retrieval system, or transmitted, in any form or by any means—electronic, mechanical, photocopying, recording, or otherwise—without prior written permission, except for brief quotations in critical reviews or articles.

Unless otherwise noted, Scripture quotations are taken from the Holy Bible: English Standard Version, copyright © 2001, Wheaton: Good News Publishers. Used by permission. All rights reserved.

Scripture quotations marked NKJV™ are taken from the New King James Version®. Copyright © 1982 by Thomas Nelson, Inc. Used by permission. All rights reserved.

ISBN
Paperback 978-1-7371956-0-3
ebook 978-1-7371956-1-0

AnglicanCompass.com

Printed in the United States of America

CONTENTS

Introduction *11*

1. Story: A Brief History of Anglicanism *17*

2. Orthodoxy: Anglican Beliefs *33*

3. Prayer: The Book of Common Prayer *47*

4. Liturgy: How Anglicans Worship *59*

5. Sacraments: Baptism and Eucharist *75*

6. Scripture: Anglicans and the Bible *87*

7. Order: Holy Orders and Structure *97*

8. Mission: Anglican Mission Today *113*

9. Charity: Embracing the Anglican Via Media *131*

Conclusion *147*

Glossary of Anglican Terms *150*

Endnotes *158*

INTRODUCTION

"There is something in the air today, something in the spirit of our age, something in the Spirit that is leading thousands, maybe millions, of people to reconsider liturgical forms of worship."

—Bishop Todd Hunter

IN AN INCREASINGLY chaotic world, no one is really interested in a church that provides a slightly different version of what the world can give them. If the church is just another vendor of services—not even a good one in some cases—what does it have that they cannot get elsewhere? Perhaps new and innovative approaches to being the church are not the answer to our problems after all. Rather than coming up with something new and trendy, many people today are hungry for a faith that is vintage and time-tested. The truth is, many contemporary people are longing for a faith that was not started yesterday and is not driven by fads or personalities.[1]

So what, if anything, could an ancient tradition offer today's world? The answer is a lot. Far from being a faith of the past, Anglicanism presents a rich spiritual tradition that has matured into a worldwide movement of Christians on every continent. The Anglican tradition offers a refreshing alternative to our postmodern world by helping us reconnect to the historic Christian faith in a way that speaks to our present age. Thousands of people across the world are embracing the Anglican tradition, which is an ancient faith that holds great promise for today's world. The fact that you're reading this book reveals that Anglicanism has sparked an interest within you in some form or fashion. I assure you, you're not alone. Today, people from various backgrounds are exploring the Anglican tradition anew.

MY JOURNEY TO ANGLICANISM

Through a long journey, I eventually found my home in the Anglican tradition. I grew up in a Baptist home and came to faith in the Pentecostal Church. I gleaned a lot from these traditions and experiences, such as being born again and filled with the Spirit. But despite these gifts, I always felt as if something were missing. What I didn't realize at the time was that I was longing to be a part of a tradition with a connection to the historic Christian faith. I found this bountiful connection in Anglicanism.

In many ways I read and prayed my way into the Anglican tradition. For years, I had devoured the writings of Anglican authors and theologians like J. I. Packer, N. T. Wright, and C. S. Lewis. You could say I was a "closet Anglican." Then one day I heard a rumor that an old friend from college and his church had become Anglican. Trinity Anglican Mission in Atlanta, Georgia, began as a Vineyard church. One day I decided to call and talk to the founding pastor, Kris McDaniel, to find out what was going on there. During our talk he suggested that I fly out to Atlanta to see what the Lord was doing at Trinity and to discern whether the Lord might be calling me to become an Anglican.

Not knowing what I was going to experience, I boarded a plane and flew out to spend a weekend at Trinity. I was moved by the liturgical worship service that brought together a beautiful blend of what some have come to call the three streams (Evangelical, Sacramental, and Charismatic).[2] But it was not until I met with Kris after the service that I became convinced this tradition was for

INTRODUCTION

me. While we spent time in his office, he said something profound. "Winfield," he said, "you've been splashing in these waters your whole ministry. There comes a time when you have to ask the Lord, 'Can I get in this stream?'" In that moment I knew I had found my home in the Anglican tradition.

I returned home sensing the Lord was calling me to be a part of the Anglican tradition. Around this time, Charles Gill, a retired Anglican priest who was a close friend and mentor, began to encourage me to reach out to Steve Wood, bishop of the Anglican Diocese of the Carolinas, about my interest in Anglicanism. In Bishop Steve, I found a spiritual leader and close friend. After some preliminary discussions and preparations, my family and I made our way to Mt. Pleasant, South Carolina, where I was ordained as a transitional deacon in the Anglican Church in North America. The service was simple, yet beautifully profound and historic. I will never forget the sense of God's presence and holiness as I made my ordination vows saying, "I, Winfield Bevins, do believe the Holy Scriptures of the Old and New Testaments to be the Word of God and to contain all things necessary to salvation, and I consequently hold myself bound to conform my life and ministry thereto, and therefore I do solemnly engage to conform to the Doctrine, Discipline and Worship of Christ as this Church has received them."[3] Only a few months after this profound experience, I was ordained as an Anglican priest and have served in this role ever since.

Becoming Anglican helped me realize that I am a part of the larger Christian family whose roots go back to the time of Christ. Too often, contemporary Christians forget that the church has existed with a rich history for two thousand years. Anglicanism helped me realize that I am not an independent contemporary Christian restricted to my own time. Rather, I am part of the larger body of Christ whose roots began not with the Reformation or the evangelical movement, but with Jesus Christ. As I've walked this new path in my life, I have met many other evangelicals who are longing for a faith that wasn't started yesterday and is not driven by fads or personalities. My story is not unique. Like so many others who have searched long and hard, I have come to embrace the richness of the Anglican way of living out the Christian faith.

ABOUT THIS BOOK

Since I became an Anglican I have had countless conversations with those who are seriously exploring Anglicanism but don't know where to start. Sometimes daily, I am asked by people, "What is Anglicanism?" As former Archbishop of Canterbury Rowan Williams said, "The word 'Anglican' begs a question at once."[4] At first glance, the Anglican tradition can seem quite complex and inaccessible to those coming from other traditions. In an effort to answer questions newcomers often have, I have written a short introduction to the Anglican tradition. It is my hope that it will be a helpful resource for everyone, regardless of what their background may be.

Maybe you are wondering, "Why another book on Anglicanism?" After all, there are endless books on the subject, many of which will be featured in the "Recommended Reading" sections of this book. However, many of them are either too academic, or written for those already within the tradition, while others are focused on all of the problems facing Anglicanism. Therefore, I have intentionally chosen a different approach, one that is simple, yet thoughtful and graciously orthodox. To borrow a phrase from my friends at Anglican Compass, I want to "help you navigate the Anglican tradition with clarity

INTRODUCTION

and charity."⁵

While I am a North American Anglican, I am writing broadly for all those who are exploring Anglicanism in different jurisdictions around the world. Whether you find yourself in New Zealand, England, North America, or Nigeria, I hope this will be a helpful introduction as you seek to navigate the rich and beautiful liturgical tradition of Anglicanism. As an author, I have the unique perspective of one who has discovered the Anglican tradition relatively recently but has been a part of it long enough to want to share it with others. I am like a person who has found a priceless treasure and, rather than keeping it all for myself, I want to share it with the world! As you read, I hope you too will discover that the Anglican way brings together the past, present, and future through a foundation built upon the "faith that was once for all delivered to the saints" (Jude 1:3).

Another reason I wrote the book is because Anglicanism has undergone major changes in the last century. In fact, Anglicanism has radically changed even in the last few years, and this book is an attempt to reflect the current realities within the worldwide Anglican Communion. Anglicanism has grown into a worldwide family of churches, which has more than 80 million followers in 161 countries, making it the third largest body of Christians in the world. Anglicans speak many languages and come from different races and cultures. The explosive growth of Anglicanism has created many new realities. For instance, there are now more Anglicans worshiping in Nigeria than in England, Canada, and the United States combined.⁶ *Simply Anglican* can be used by individuals or small groups who are exploring the beliefs and practices of the Anglican faith. I have also included questions in the back of the book that can be used for personal reflection or group study. You will notice sidebars in each chapter with a quote from the experience of someone who was new to the Anglican way.[7] In keeping with the Anglican emphasis upon prayer, I have concluded each chapter with a prayer from the *Book of Common Prayer*. Finally, throughout the book you will meet other pilgrims who have embraced the Anglican tradition. Wherever you are on your journey, I hope you will find this introduction to the Anglican tradition both encouraging and helpful.

CHAPTER 1
STORY: A BRIEF HISTORY OF ANGLICANISM

> "I had always felt life first as a story: and if there is a story there is a storyteller." —G. K. Chesterton

EVERYONE LOVES A GOOD STORY. Story relates truths through painting a world, drawing the reader into its landscape. There is something captivating about a good story, and all great stories echo the one great Story: the Bible's Story of God's redemptive plan for humankind throughout the ages. God is the great Storyteller, and history is one grand narrative of God's redemptive love for lost humanity. It begins with creation and climaxes with God sending His Son, Jesus Christ, to die for our sins and rise victorious over evil and death. For centuries, authors and painters have used their talents to depict this narrative through art and song.

> *"Then I found my place in the Anglican tradition, and it was a place that felt safe. It's certainly not a perfect place. But it's a place that's securely rooted in hundreds and hundreds of years of tradition that spans both time and space. It's a tradition that transcends cultural fads. It's a tradition that embraces daily, weekly, and yearly patterns that become a stable and constant rhythm in the Christian's life."* —Drew Haltom[1]

God's Story helps us understand His true nature by focusing on the message of His redemptive plan rather than on bare historical facts. History is full of amazing tales about great men and women of faith whom God used to change the course of history and who influenced the world with the Word of God, but these historical figures all point to the larger purpose of God. Sadly, we live in a story-deprived world in which people don't know where they came from or where they are going. We tend to focus on the now at the expense of the eternal. Many contemporary Christians have historical amnesia and are missing vital aspects of the faith that are necessary for spiritual growth and maturity. The result is that we have no roots and therefore don't know who we really are. In many ways, we have lost our story.

Our lack of historical awareness can be remedied by opening the pages of church history and returning to the roots of faith that have nourished believers since the time of Christ. Christians are beginning to rediscover that church history has much to teach us about living out the Christian faith. Through a beautiful blending of ancient foundations and vision for the future, the Anglican tradition offers a refreshing alternative to our postmodern world by helping us reconnect to the larger Christian narrative in a way that speaks to our present age. Anglicanism has a rich history that can help us rediscover our own place within the larger Story of God.

In this chapter, I want to offer a brief introduction to and overview of the history of Anglicanism. The Anglican tradition traces its roots back to the time of the Roman Empire when a Christian church first came into existence in the British Isles. Anglican actually means "English," and refers to the church's place of origin. The term "Anglican church" is simply a translation of the Latin phrase *ecclesia anglicana* and refers to the church in England. According to legend, Christianity first came to England through Joseph of Arimathea, although this cannot be known for certain. Church fathers Tertullian and Origen both spoke of a church in England around AD 200; Saint Alban's execution in AD 209 represents the first Christian martyrdom in the British Isles; and in AD 314, Britain sent three bishops to the Council of Arles. As you can see, not only have Christians inhabited the British Isles since the third century, they have also actively contributed to the history of Christianity since that time.

Of course, the British Isles include more than just England. When most of us think of Ireland, we think about green rolling hills and countryside covered in grass. But few people know that more than fifteen hundred years ago, this island birthed one of the most influential movements in the history of the Christian church. In fact, some scholars argue that the Celtic Christians, who called Ireland their home, contributed to the preservation of western civilization. Christianity spread throughout the British Isles under the leadership of Celtic missionaries like Patrick (387–493), who baptized thousands of people, ordained hundreds of ministers, and helped plant hundreds of churches throughout the British Isles.

Christianity continued to spread throughout the British Isles like wildfire under the gifted leadership of monks such as Columba (521–597) in Iona, and Aidan in Lindisfarne (651 AD). Contrary to common stereotypes, these monasteries did not house monastic recluses. Rather, they became spiritual centers and discipleship-training hubs that commissioned missionaries throughout Western Europe. The churches and monasteries of this movement became some of the most influential missionary centers in all of Europe.[2] Missionaries went out from Ireland to spread the gospel throughout the world. These Irish monasteries helped preserve the Christian faith during the dark ages.

AUGUSTINE AND THE MIDDLE AGES

An important step in the history of the English church happened in 596 when Pope Gregory the Great sent one of his assistants, a Benedictine monk named Augustine, to evangelize the Anglo-Saxons. Due to his influence, many consider Augustine the "Apostle to the English." He eventually arrived in Kent (the southeast corner of England) in 597 with a team of monks. There, King Aethelbert, whose wife already practiced Christianity, allowed Augustine and his team to settle and preach among the people. Augustine eventually succeeded in converting the king and many others to the Christian faith. Often when a king converted, his subjects would follow, and this case was no different. This unique connection between king and church continued throughout the ages and remains a crucial historical tenet to understanding the complex relationship between the church and state in the Church of England.

Augustine became the first Archbishop of Canterbury and established a center for Christianity in Britain. From that time onward, the Archbishop of Canterbury has been honored and respected as the spiritual leader of the Church of England and the worldwide Anglican Communion. In a letter, Pope Gregory wisely counseled Augustine to allow room for the English church to retain its own distinctiveness: "For things are not to be loved for the sake of places but places for the sake of good things. Select, therefore, from every church the things that are devout, religious and upright, and when you have, as it were, combined them into one body, let the minds of the English be trained therein."[3]

Augustine lived during the beginning of the medieval time period, which lasted from the 5th to the 15th century. This time period was a tumultuous time that marked the beginning of the collapse of the Roman Empire and preceded the Renaissance and the Age of Discovery. During this period, the Catholic Church represented the single most powerful institution and became the main stabilizing force in all of Western Europe, including England. In addition to being a major religious influence, the Church also provided significant secular leadership as well by playing a key role in learning and the general welfare of the people. For the common person, the Church's rituals marked important moments in an individual's life including baptism, confirmation, marriage, holy orders, and the last rites before burial.

It was also during this time that division between the Orthodox Christian Church in the East and the Roman Catholic Church in the West began. At the heart of this split was the Roman Catholic Church's insistence on the Pope as being the head of the Church as well as the emergence of differing views on the person and work of the Holy Spirit. Sadly, the two branches of Christianity reached an impasse and permanently split in 1054.

Because of the Catholic Church's power, the middle ages represent a time of many abuses such as the selling of indulgences, through which people could purchase the remission of the temporal punishment in purgatory. The church abused these indulgences through unrestricted sales so that they could help pay off the Roman Catholic Church's debts and also fund building projects like St. Peter's Basilica in Rome. It was the sale and abuses of indulgences and other excesses of the Catholic Church that helped spark the fires of the Reformation.

In spite of what many have people have claimed, the middle ages were not completely "dark ages." In fact, the medieval time period offered many contributions to the faith that would eventually bear the name Anglicanism. For instance, a number of the great cathedrals in England and the rest of Europe, including Canterbury and Westminster, were constructed during this time period.

Another development from the Medieval time period that was closely associated with the cathedrals was the emergence of the great English choral tradition. This beautiful musical tradition owes its existence to the roots of the monastic past when monks, sometimes joined by other singers, would chant the daily offices. Today, cathedral choirs are made up of both adult singers and children who are professionally trained and sing several times a week in services around the world. Sitting in one of these beautiful choral services is like stepping back into the Medieval past and offers contemporary Christians a living connection to the history of the church.

THE REFORMATION COMES TO ENGLAND

While the fires of the Protestant Reformation were sweeping across Europe, a different kind of Reformation was under way in England. At first, the English Reformation was political as much as it was theological. Henry VIII wanted an annulment of his marriage to Catherine of Aragon, who could not produce him a male heir. The Pope refused to grant an annulment and Henry sought to break ties with Rome. In 1533, Henry selected a young priest and theologian who was broadly sympathetic to his cause, Thomas Cranmer, as Archbishop of Canterbury. This began an unusual relationship between Cranmer and King Henry. The two men used one another to accomplish their own personal goals and ambitions. The King wanted to remarry and Cranmer wanted to see Reformation come to England. The break with Rome was enacted through a series of acts of Parliament passed between 1532 and 1534, among them the

STORY: A BRIEF HISTORY OF ANGLICANISM

1534 Act of Supremacy, which declared that Henry was the "Supreme Head on earth of the Church of England." This event marked the official beginning of the Church of England.

It is important to note that the Reformation in England was not just about King Henry's many marriages (six in all). Rather, the English Reformation was, in part, associated with the wider religious and political reformation movement that affected all of Europe during this period. Thomas Cranmer vigorously worked to see the Reformation come to England. Under the leadership of Cranmer, the Church of England began to embrace elements of the Reformation throughout England, but still retained many of the historic practices of the Catholic Church. Cranmer carefully danced around the politics of his position but still enacted a number of reforms in England. After Henry's death, Cranmer more fully pursued the Reformation in England under Henry's son Edward VI.

The Reformation in England has been called "Reformed Catholicism" because it embraced theology of the Reformation while at the same time it retained many of the time-honored practices of the historic Catholic tradition. This complex juxtaposition between the Reformed and Catholic streams is one of the unique dynamics of Anglicanism that will be further explained and explored throughout the remainder of the book. These two streams will provide lenses that will help the reader understand the development of Anglicanism in contrast to other Reformation traditions such as Lutheranism, Calvinism, and the Radical Reformers, which completely separated in both theology and practice from the Catholic Church.

Cranmer realized two of his greatest achievements in 1549 and 1553. First, he was instrumental in producing one of the most widely read English religious books, second only to the King James Bible.

It is known as the Book of Common Prayer (often referred to as the "BCP" or "Prayer Book"). In 1549, he helped organize the Book of Common Prayer in the English language. Cranmer and a committee of twelve others compiled the Prayer Book from various sources, including ancient prayers of the early church, Catholic and Orthodox liturgies, and private devotions of the Middle Ages. They translated many of these sources into the English language. Later, in June of 1553, Edward VI gave his agreement to Cranmer's initial Forty-Two Articles of Religion, which would eventually become a foundational document for Anglican doctrine and beliefs.

> *"When Kris and I and our two children, Laura and Lukas, moved to Nottingham England we were invited to attend St Peter's Church (Toton) with a curate named John Corrie. We had never used The Book of Common Prayer but on the very first Sunday, along with wondering why the music didn't have notes and worrying about when to stand or sit, I heard for the first time the words of the collects, those weekly prayers recited, often from rote memory. My born again past met the living faith of living words in the collects and I was overwhelmed. And have been ever since."* —SCOT MCKNIGHT[4]

A BRIEF RETURN TO ROME

After Edward VI's death, Cranmer supported Lady Jane Grey as Edward's successor. Unfortunately for Cranmer, her reign lasted only nine days before she was deposed (July 10–19, 1553). Following Lady Jane Grey's reign, Queen "Bloody" Mary ascended to the throne and tried Cranmer for treason, imprisoning him in September 1553

These were dangerous times to be a Protestant in England. Cranmer's

STORY: A BRIEF HISTORY OF ANGLICANISM

fellow English reformers, Nicholas Ridley and Hugh Latimer, were burned at the stake in Oxford on October 16, 1555. As he was being tied to the stake, Ridley prayed, "O heavenly Father, I give unto thee most hearty thanks, that thou hast called me to be a professor of thee, even unto death; I beseech thee, Lord God, have mercy on this realm of England, and deliver it from all her enemies." As the flames quickly rose around them, Latimer encouraged Ridley, "Be of good comfort, Mr. Ridley, and play the man! We shall this day light such a candle by God's grace, in England, as I trust never shall be put out."

In March 1554, Cranmer defended his religious views against a delegation appointed by the queen. Subsequently, the Roman Catholic Church condemned his views as heretical and commanded him to recant his beliefs and declare his support for Catholicism. In an interesting turn of events, Cranmer recanted in private. However, on March 21, 1556, Cranmer was to do the same in public, but he refused and was burned at the stake as a heretic. At his execution, he withdrew his forced confession and proclaimed the truth of the Protestant faith. He placed his hand in the fire, the hand with which he had falsely signed his renouncement of his beliefs, and declared, "This hand hath offended!"[6]

The Reformation in England ultimately cost Cranmer his life, but his legacy remains. Despite his recantations, he stands out as one of the most influential leaders of the English Reformation. He helped bring the Protestant Reformation to the Church of England, and he co-authored one of the most beautiful and important devotional books ever composed. To this day, millions around the world are still reaping the harvest from his endeavors, which were foundational to the Church of England and to the creation of the Book of Common Prayer.

POST-REFORMATION DEVELOPMENTS

Another important development in Anglicanism happened during the reign of Elizabeth I (1533–1603). Elizabeth was the daughter of Henry VIII and Anne Boleyn. She became Queen of England in 1558 during the tumultuous time when religious differences between Protestant and Catholic factions threatened the stability of England. Her reign played a crucial role in the future of Anglicanism and became known as the "Elizabethan Settlement." During her time as queen, Elizabeth sought to find an inclusive middle way between Protestant and Catholic views in order to bring the English people together.

Several events foundational to the development of the Church of England occurred during the reign of Elizabeth I. The first of these came in 1559 when the Act of Supremacy took effect and proclaimed Elizabeth to be the supreme governor of the realm in all spiritual, ecclesiastical, and temporal matters. With this statement, the Church of England officially broke ties with the Roman Catholic Church. Along with this proclamation, the 1552 Prayer Book, a modified version of the Book of Common Prayer, was issued under the Act of Uniformity of 1559 and included a number of significant changes that reflected the middle way between the Protestant and Catholic extremes. Later in 1563, a convocation of the church established the Thirty-Nine Articles of Religion as a foundational statement of Anglican beliefs (we will discuss these articles in greater depth in Chapter 2). The Elizabethan settlement proved to be an important step in bringing the different religious groups together in England through a "middle way" (*via media*), which has become an important hallmark of the Anglican tradition.

Two important Anglican theologians from this time who are also worth noting are Bishop John Jewel and Richard Hooker. John Jewel (1522–1571), bishop of Salisbury, helped to defend the English Reformation from Roman Catholics. In his *Apology for the Church of England*, he argued against the supremacy of the pope and stated that the Roman Catholic Church, not the Church of England, had departed from the faith. Richard Hooker (1554–1600), who is still considered one of the most important theologians in the Anglican tradition, defended Anglicanism from the Puritans. He sought to defend the Episcopal form of government over and against the Presbyterian model of the Puritans.

The Puritans in the 16th and 17th centuries believed that the Reformation in England did not go far enough and they sought to "purify" the Church of England from all Roman Catholic practices. The clash between the Puritans and the established Church of England eventually led to a civil war, in which the Puritans attempted to establish a theocratic form of government. The outcome of the war led to the trial and execution of Charles I, the exile of his son Charles II, and the replacement of the English monarchy with a commonwealth led by Oliver Cromwell. During this time, the bishop-led Church of England was disbanded and the Book of Common Prayer was in general disuse. However, the Puritan reign was short-lived and, after Cromwell's death in 1658, it began to fall apart.

In 1660, Charles II came back into power and the Church of England was reestablished. Several significant things happened in 1662. First, the Parliament passed the Act of Uniformity that required all clergy to adhere to the rites and ceremonies of the Book of Common Prayer. This led to the "Great Ejection" where two thousand Puritan clergy were forced out of their positions. Second, the Book of Common Prayer was revised. This 1662 edition of the Prayer Book is still considered authoritative to this day and churches around the world continue to use it. Of special importance, this version included an *ordinal* (ordination rite) for ordaining bishops, priests, and deacons. This final edition completed the development of the classic Anglican Formularies (foundational documents): the 1662 Book of Common Prayer, the Ordinal, the Books of Homilies, and the Thirty-Nine Articles of Religion.

ANGLICANISM IN THE MODERN ERA

The 19th-century in England saw the rise of the Industrial Revolution, which brought with it a new set of challenges and opportunities that the world had never seen before. It was a time of great change and upheaval in the church and culture alike. The spirit of the age caused many to rethink the importance of the church's role in society. Many Christians fought to end slavery, restrict child labor, and champion women's rights.

> *"The liturgy continues to ground me. Whether it's by its prayers or by its lectionary readings, or by how it has created a rhythm of life, I feel that for once in my life I know what solid ground feels like. My solid ground is not just faith, it's not just liturgy, it's not just Scriptures. It's all those, but it's also the shoulders of the saints that have gone before, the shoulders of the saints living now, and (mysteriously) it's the shoulders of the saints that will come after me."* —DEMELZA RAMIREZ

Many Christians in the 19th-century began to ask the question, "Should the church embrace the advances of contemporary society, or should it seek to remain faithful to its historic foundation?"

During this time, an influential group known as the "Oxford Movement" sought to recover the Catholic thought and practice of the Church of England. Centered at the University of Oxford, the proponents of the Oxford Movement believed that the Anglican Church was by history a truly "catholic" church. They believed that Anglicanism was one of three historic branches of Christianity, including Eastern Orthodoxy and Roman Catholicism.

Key leaders of the movement were John Keble (1792–1866), a clergyman and poet; Edward Pusey (1800–82), a clergyman and professor at Oxford; and John Henry Newman (1801–90), a clergyman who eventually became a convert to Roman Catholicism and a cardinal. The ideas of the movement were published in 90 *Tracts for the Times*, 24 of which were written by Newman, who edited the entire series. The *Tracts* promoted a recovery of the Catholic tradition within Anglicanism. Supporters of the *Tracts* were known as Tractarians. Although Newman joined the Roman Catholic Church in 1845, Keble and Pusey remained active Anglican leaders of the Oxford Movement throughout their lifetime.

In time, the ideas of the Oxford Movement spread throughout England and into other provinces. According to Michael Ramsey, "The Oxford Movement initiated a deep spiritual and intellectual revival in the Anglican Church."[7] The Oxford Movement helped Anglicanism recover many of the lost practices of the One, Holy, Catholic, and Apostolic Church. The contributions of the Oxford Movement can still be seen in Anglican churches around the world today in a variety of ways, including the use of vestments and ritual, the importance of ordained ministry, the central place of the Eucharist in worship, the establishment of Anglican monastic communities, and a strong emphasis on education for clergy.

It is important to remember that many have criticized the "Victorian" church (named after Queen Victoria, who reigned from 1837–1901) for issues related to colonization and British imperialism. While there is certainly truth in this, this season also gave rise to great advances in world missions. Anglican mission organizations like the Society for Promoting Christian Knowledge (SPCK), the Society for the Propagation of the Gospel in Foreign Parts (SPG), and the Church Missionary Society (CMS) helped spread the gospel throughout the world and sowed the seeds for what is now the worldwide Anglican Communion.

GLOBAL ANGLICANISM

Today a new chapter in the Anglican story is being written. There was a time when people associated Anglicanism with the West. However, that is no longer the case. Although it started in England, Anglicanism has become one of the world's most multicultural and multi-ethnic churches, having grown into a worldwide family of churches. Anglicanism has more than eighty million adherents spreading across 165 countries, making it the third largest body of Christians in the world.[8] Located across the globe, Anglicans speak many languages and hail from different races and cultures, but are united by their love of the gospel of Jesus Christ and the use of the Book of Common Prayer. According to Phillip Jenkins, "By 2050, the global total of Anglicans will be approaching 150 million, of whom only a tiny minority will be White Europeans."

In keeping with the wider Christian trend, the Global South movement represents the greatest growth in the Anglican Communion in recent years. Anglican growth on the continents of Asia, Africa, and South America has exploded. Today, it is the churches of the Global South who are helping to lead the future direction of the Anglican Communion.

CONCLUSION

In conclusion, over the ages the Anglican tradition has produced some of the world's greatest Christian thinkers, writers, and leaders such as Bishop Jeremy Taylor, John Donne, John and Charles Wesley, Charles Simeon, J. C. Ryle, Jane Austen, C. S. Lewis, Dorothy L. Sayers, William Temple, and Festo Kivengere, to name a few.[10] With more than fifteen hundred years of rich history, this ancient tradition still has the power to speak to our contemporary world with a faith that is relevant for a new generation. Those of us who are part of the Anglican tradition are writing the next chapter in the story. As we shall see in the coming chapters, Anglicanism advocates participation in a vibrant global faith that engages the world and transforms lives with the gospel of Jesus Christ. In the next chapter we will explore what Anglicans believe.

DISCUSSION QUESTIONS

1. We live in a world that devalues tradition and lacks historical awareness. After reading this chapter, why do you think that history matters to the church today?

2. What are the implications of tracing the Anglican heritage through the centuries?

3. What elements, time periods, or characters seem to be especially significant in the history of Anglicanism?

4. How has Anglicanism adapted and changed through the ages?

CLOSING PRAYER

O Lord our God, by your Son Jesus Christ you called your apostles and sent them forth to preach the Gospel to the nations: We bless your holy Name for your servant Augustine, first Archbishop of Canterbury, whose labors in propagating your Church among the English people we commemorate today; and we pray that all whom you call and send may do your will, and bide your time, and see your glory; through Jesus Christ our Lord, who lives and reigns with you and the Holy Spirit, one God, for ever and ever. Amen.[11]

RECOMMENDED READING

A History of the Church in England by John Moorman

A History of the Episcopal Church by Robert W. Pritchard

Christianity: The First Three Thousand Years by Diarmaid MacCulloch

Ecclesiastical History of the English People by The Venerable Bede

Glorious Companions: Five Centuries of Anglican Spirituality by Richard H. Schmidt

The Oxford History of Anglicanism, Volumes I–V

The Study of Anglicanism edited by Stephen Sykes, John Booty, and Jonathan Knight

Thomas Cranmer: A Life by Diarmaid MacCulloch

CHAPTER 2
ORTHODOXY: ANGLICAN BELIEFS

"The 'Anglican' movement in the sixteenth century was a return to the pure and simple faith of Christianity as embodied in the Holy Scriptures." —W. H. Griffith Thomas

---

WHAT WE BELIEVE shapes our identity, and ultimately, who we are. Singer-songwriter Rich Mullins affirmed this in an older song called "Creed." In the words of the song, he writes: "And I believe what I believe is what makes me what I am. I did not make it; no, it is making me. It is the very truth of God, and not the invention of any man." Orthodoxy means "right belief," and for Christianity, a right belief is a belief that agrees with the whole of Scripture and the teachings of Jesus and the apostles. This is especially true regarding the core doctrines of the Trinity and the Church. What makes Christian orthodoxy stand apart in our postmodern world is its clear statements of what we believe, and the commitment to hold to these beliefs regardless of the relativism we find in the world. While others may abandon their beliefs for the latest trends, Christians are rooted, holding firm, concrete beliefs about the Triune God: Father, Son, and Holy Spirit.

Our orthodoxy—right beliefs—are important for discipleship because orthodoxy is directly connected to *orthopraxy*, our "right action." The practical application of a belief is an action taken in response to or based on that belief. This is why what we believe about God matters immensely. What we believe about God influences how we think, pray, worship, and, ultimately, how we live. No, we are not all called to be professional theologians, but every Christian has a responsibility to know what they believe for themselves. You can't worship what you don't know. Anglicans understand that this interaction between belief and practice is paramount.

> *"'We believe in one God, the Father Almighty, maker of heaven and earth...'" As I said the words, there was a dim flicker of hope beneath the layers of exhaustion. I heard my voice blending in with the voices of those around me, saying words that Christians have said for hundreds of years, reaffirming my faith in the Triune God despite my circumstances and despite my feelings. And as the syllables rolled off my tongue, my weary spirit began to revive."* —EMILY MCGOWIN[1]

So, what do Anglicans believe? In one sense, Anglicans have no distinct beliefs of their own. Anglicans simply believe what Christians have espoused since the times of the historic creeds and councils. These essentials are what C. S. Lewis had in mind when he wrote *Mere Christianity* in order "to explain and defend the belief that has been common to nearly all Christians at all times."[2] Since the earliest of times, Christians have believed the teachings of the Bible and recited the creeds during times of prayer and worship to remind them of the faith they professed, the faith handed down to the apostles and guarded by the church to the present day.

However, in another important sense, Anglicans *do* have a unique set of beliefs that embraces the best of the ancient Christian faith and the Protestant Reformation. In an article titled "Is There an 'Anglican Understanding' of the New Testament?" Professor Wesley Hill said the following about Anglican beliefs:

> Anglicanism's chief glory is to present and embody the faith of the church catholic—downwind of the Reformation, with a robust understanding of justification by faith in tow—in such a way that Anglicans may be confident that they are adhering to the same apostolic teaching and inhabiting the same ecclesial order as their earliest forebears in the faith did. . . . We are distinctive precisely by aiming not to be distinctive. Our theology is the theology of the early church, the era of the Fathers, the best of the medieval world and the Reformation—all set decently on the table in our prayer book and other formularies.[3]

Rather than reinventing the faith, Anglicanism reminds us that we need to get back to the foundational truths of Christianity, back to orthodoxy. I believe every generation of believers must revisit the faith and doctrines of the early church as found in the Holy Scriptures and the historic creeds. In our time, these truths and doctrines sharply contrast with the postmodern mood of our culture, providing a new or young Christian with a substantial foundation upon which to stand. The mission of the church is to engage a changing world with an ancient faith that is relevant and fresh for each generation. It's about communicating clearly and calling each generation to the solid foundation of orthodoxy.

Anglicanism has common beliefs, a corporate confession, and a corporate affirmation of faith that forms our faith and gives us a foundation to stand in the midst of a changing world. In the following pages we will explore the common beliefs that form Anglicans worldwide. This chapter will offer a brief introduction and overview of the foundational Anglican standards for understanding Christian faith as rooted in the Holy Scriptures, the historic creeds of the Christian faith, the Thirty-Nine Articles of Religion, and a unique way of learning theology called *catechesis*.

SCRIPTURE AND THE CREEDS

Anglican Christianity is unified by its center, not by its boundaries. In particular, the three creeds of the church (the Apostles' Creed, Nicene Creed, and Athanasian Creed) constitute the core of Anglican belief. But what exactly is a creed? A creed is a brief statement of faith used to summarize Biblical teaching, clarify doctrinal points, and distinguish truth from error. The word *creed* comes from the Latin word *credo,* meaning, "I believe." The Bible contains a number of creed-like passages (see Deuteronomy 6:4–9; 1 Corinthians 8:6; 15:3–4; 1 Timothy 3:16).

The historic creeds offer us a concise summary of authentic Christian beliefs. They contain essential Christian doctrines (e.g., the divinity of Christ, the virgin birth, the Trinity) common to the majority of Christians. It is through our common faith in these essentials that Anglicans can seek unity with other Christians. Our creeds guard the faith, but they do not limit the leading of the Holy Spirit. The common ground of faith established by the creeds allows us to move forward together into the world to fulfill the mission of God. Because of their importance, the creeds fill the pages of the Book of Common Prayer and shape its prayers, liturgies, ceremonies, and catechism. In many ways, the creeds act as an anchor that provides a doctrinal foundation for Anglicans everywhere.

The Apostles' Creed represents the most concise creed observed by Anglicans. As the early church spread, it needed a practical statement of faith to help believers focus on the most important doctrines of their Christian faith. The creed is traditionally attributed to the apostles, even though there is no historical justification for this belief. However, the Apostles' Creed accurately reflects the teaching of the apostles—the apostolic faith. The earliest form of the Apostles' Creed appeared around the second century, and it seems to have assumed its final form in the eighth century.

As the church continued to grow, heresies also grew, and the early Christians needed even more clarification in order to define the boundaries of the faith. In the early 300s, controversy arose over the divinity of Jesus Christ. At the request of Emperor Constantine, Christian bishops from across the East and the West met at the town of Nicaea, near Constantinople. In AD 325 they wrote an expanded creed called the Creed of Nicaea, which was finalized in its current form at the Council of Constantinople in AD 381. Along with the Apostles' Creed, Christians widely accept the Nicene Creed as a statement of true Christian orthodoxy. The Anglican church employs the Apostles' Creed as the statement of faith during baptism and Morning and Evening Prayer, while the Nicene Creed is recited in the service of Holy Communion.

Finally, the Athanasian Creed was an attempt to protect the church from heresies that denied the humanity and divinity of Jesus and from false teachings related to the doctrine of the Trinity. Although it was most likely composed at some point during the fifth century, the Athanasian Creed is traditionally ascribed to Athanasius (293–373), a defender of orthodox teaching about Jesus Christ against the heresy of Arianism, which maintained that Jesus was a created being, not God. The Athanasian Creed offers a detailed statement of the doctrine of the Trinity: "That we worship one God in Trinity, and Trinity in Unity; Neither confounding the persons nor dividing the substance. For there is one person of the Father, another of the Son, and another of the Holy Spirit.[4]

Our creeds are not static statements about the Christian faith; rather they offer the church a dynamic means of unity in the essentials of our common faith. With the creeds as a foundation, we can be open to the diversity that permeates the various church traditions. Our unity in essentials gives us common ground, while our diversity provides us the means for various dialogues and opinions within the body of Christ. With the creeds as our foundation, the church of the past can speak to the present, and the church of the present can reach into the future through a common faith and a common prayer.

THIRTY-NINE ARTICLES OF RELIGION

The Thirty-Nine Articles of Religion represent another pillar of Anglican beliefs. First developed over the course of the Reformation era, the Articles came into their final form and number in 1571 during the reign of Queen Elizabeth I and under the direction of Archbishop Matthew Parker. The church never intended for the Articles to be a comprehensive statement of the Christian faith, but originally thought of them as a way to clarify the position of the Church of England against the Roman Catholic Church and also certain continental Reformers.

The Thirty-Nine Articles of Religion are among the finest statements of the faith produced during the time of the Reformation and remain relevant for today's world. Here is a list of the articles, for an idea of their content:

1. Of Faith in the Holy Trinity.
2. Of Christ the Son of God.
3. Of his going down into Hell.
4. Of his Resurrection.
5. Of the Holy Ghost.
6. Of the Sufficiency of the Scriptures.
7. Of the Old Testament.
8. Of the Three Creeds.
9. Of Original or Birth-sin.
10. Of Free-Will.
11. Of Justification.
12. Of Good Works.
13. Of Works before Justification.
14. Of Works of Supererogation.
15. Of Christ alone without Sin.
16. Of Sin after Baptism.
17. Of Predestination and Election.
18. Of obtaining Salvation by Christ.
19. Of the Church.
20. Of the Authority of the Church.
21. Of the Authority of General Councils.
22. Of Purgatory.
23. Of Ministering in the Congregation.
24. Of speaking in the Congregation.
25. Of the Sacraments.
26. Of the Unworthiness of Ministers.

27. Of Baptism.
28. Of the Lord's Supper.
29. Of the Wicked which eat not the Body of Christ.
30. Of both kinds.
31. Of Christ's one Oblation.
32. Of the Marriage of Priests.
33. Of Excommunicate Persons.
34. Of the Traditions of the Church.
35. Of the Homilies.
36. Of Consecrating of Ministers.
37. Of Civil Magistrates.
38. Of Christian men's Goods.
39. Of a Christian man's Oath.[5]

According to theologian Gerald Bray, the Thirty-Nine Articles can be divided into three distinct categories: Catholic doctrines, Protestant doctrines, and Anglican doctrines. The Catholic doctrines are found in Articles 1–8 and deal with the Holy Trinity (1–5), the Holy Scriptures (6–7), and the ancient creeds (8). The Protestant doctrines are found in Articles 9–34, which deal with salvation (9–10), justification by faith (11–14), the Christian life (15–18), the church (19–22), the ministry (23–24), the sacraments (25–31), and church discipline (32–34). Finally, the Anglican doctrines are found in articles 35–37 and deal with the Homilies (or key sermons), the threefold order of ministry (bishops, priests, and deacons), and the relationship of church and state. The last two articles (38–39) are not specifically Anglican but deal with matters of civil government.[6]

A key to understanding the overall tenor of the Thirty-Nine Articles is the doctrine of God's saving grace. Article XI says, "We are accounted righteous before God, only for the merit of our Lord and Saviour Jesus Christ by Faith, and not for our own works or deservings: Wherefore, that we are justified by Faith only is a most wholesome Doctrine, and very full of comfort."

In summing up the importance of the Articles, Bishop J. C. Ryle reminded Anglicans, "Doctrines such as those set forth in the Articles are the only doctrines which are life, and health, and strength, and peace. Let us never be ashamed of laying hold of them, maintaining them, and making them our own. Those doctrines are the religion of the Bible and of the Church of England!"[7]

CHICAGO-LAMBETH QUADRILATERAL

A final way to identify what Anglicans believe is found in the Chicago-Lambeth Quadrilateral, which originally functioned as a means of unity among Christians. It addresses the Scriptures, creeds, sacraments, and the historic episcopate (governance of the church by bishops). Many Anglicans look to the Quadrilateral as a way to establish common ground among fellow Anglicans and other Christians. There were even hopes at one time that the Quadrilateral might serve as a way to reunite the different streams of the Christian church. The House of Bishops originally approved the Quadrilateral at the 1886 General Convention in Chicago, and the bishops of the Anglican Communion at the Lambeth Conference of 1888 subsequently approved it with modifications. Here are the four points the Chicago-Lambeth Quadrilateral proclaims:

1. The Holy Scriptures of the Old and New Testaments, as "containing all things necessary to salvation," and as being the rule and ultimate standard of faith.

2. The Apostles' Creed, as the Baptismal Symbol; and the Nicene Creed, as the sufficient statement of the Christian faith.

3. The two Sacraments ordained by Christ Himself—Baptism and the Supper of the Lord—ministered with unfailing use of Christ's words of Institution, and of the elements ordained by Him.

4. The Historic Episcopate, locally adapted in the methods of its administration to the varying needs of the nations and peoples called of God into the Unity of His Church.[8]

According to the Quadrilateral, these four things are the minimum requirements that need to be in place for the divided branches of Christ's Church to reunite.

ANGLICAN CATECHESIS

You've now seen how the tenets of the Anglican faith were formed, but you may be asking, "How do Anglicans practice these beliefs?" Anglicans emphasize making disciples and teaching others the basics of the Christian faith through *catechesis*. The Greek word for "instruct" or "teach" is *katecheo*, from which we get our English word "catechize." Catechesis is the process of instructing believers both young and old in the basics of the Christian faith. Typically using a question-and-answer format, catechisms are basic summaries of the biblical and creedal teaching of the church and are used to ensure that all members of the church understand the essentials of the faith for themselves. Catechisms are not a pass-or-fail, fill-in-the-blank test, but an invitation to learn the doctrines of God's goodness and grace. Using a catechism involves vital learning, ongoing reflection, and discussion within the community of faith, and has been an essential part of the church's discipleship for centuries.

Catechesis goes back to the 3rd century with the Didascalia Apostolorum (Teaching of the Apostles), which called for a three-year period of catechesis. Augustine of Hippo (353–430) also used catechesis to instruct new believers. Author J. I. Packer reminded us, "Richard Baxter, John Owen, Charles Spurgeon, and countless other pastors and leaders saw catechesis as one of their most obvious and basic pastoral duties."[9] Among these classic Reformation catechisms was the Anglican Catechism (1549), included in the first Book of Common Prayer. Recently, J. I. Packer has issued a call for the church to rediscover the lost art of catechesis. In their book, *Grounded in the Gospel: Building Believers the Old-Fashioned Way*, Packer and Gary Parrett explore the church's need to make catechesis an important part of its life once again. Catechesis, according to Packer and Parrett, "is the church's ministry of grounding and growing God's people in the gospel and its implications for doctrine, devotion, duty and delight."[10]

So, why use catechisms today? Aren't they outdated or irrelevant in the postmodern world? While rooted in times and cultures past, catechisms are important because they provide an outline of the essentials of the faith that is universal for all Christians, regardless of denomination or affiliation. Many Christians today are rediscovering the need for and the benefits of using a good catechism. Both new and established churches can benefit from using catechisms. Individuals, families, and small groups can all employ catechisms based upon their varying structures.

If you decide to utilize a catechism for yourself, I would encourage you to allow yourself time to ponder each question, reflect on the answer, and let this dialogue, whether with others or within yourself, speak to your head and your heart. Once you get the hang of using it, you can begin to use a more in-depth catechism or even write one of your own. Remember, the point is not to be slavishly tied to the past, but to learn and apply the principle of using questions and answers for helping Christians learn the essentials of the Christian faith.

If you would like a place to start, I would recommend the new catechism of the Anglican Church in North America, *To Be a Christian: An Anglican Catechism*, which is now available in both print and downloadable forms.[11] This catechism is designed as a resource for the renewal of Anglican catechetical practice and follows the essential structure of classic catechetical instruction: the Apostles' Creed, the Lord's Prayer, and the Ten Commandments. It is ideal for new and existing churches to instruct and disciple new believers in the one, holy, catholic, and apostolic faith.

In closing, Anglicans believe doctrine and devotion belong together. While doctrine can seem stuffy, boring, and useless, when grasped personally it becomes surprisingly devotional. Doctrine helps us know more about a living God. A study of God can profoundly deepen our faith and strengthen our relationship with Him. The more we know about Him, the more we love and worship Him—and vice-versa. Think about it: we cannot worship what we do not know. There is an old Latin phrase "*lex orandi, lex credendi*," which is roughly translated as "the law of praying is the law of believing." This reminds us that prayer shapes our beliefs, and our beliefs ultimately shape our prayer. To know what Anglicans believe you must come and worship with us. In the words of Archbishop Michael Ramsey, "Yes, here are our articles, but here is our Prayer

Book as well—come and pray with us, come and worship with us, and that is how you will understand what we stand for."[12]

DISCUSSION QUESTIONS

1. What significance do the historic Christian creeds have for today?

2. How have Anglicans retained the historic essentials of the Christian faith, while also embracing aspects of the Reformation?

3. How were the Thirty-Nine Articles of Religion a unique blend of Catholic, Reformation, and Anglican doctrines?

4. What is unique about the Chicago-Lambeth Quadrilateral, and how might it function as a way to unite Christians from other traditions?

CLOSING PRAYER

Almighty and everlasting God, you have given to us your servants grace, by the confession of a true faith, to acknowledge the glory of the eternal Trinity, and in the power of your divine Majesty to worship the Unity: Keep us steadfast in this faith and worship, and bring us at last to see you in your one and eternal glory, O Father; who with the Son and the Holy Spirit live and reign, one God, for ever and ever. Amen.[13]

RECOMMENDED READING

After You Believe: Why Christian Character Matters by N. T. Wright

Basic Christianity by John Stott

Christian Theology: An Introduction (sixth edition),
by Alister E. McGrath

Grounded in the Gospel: Building Believers the Old-Fashioned Way
by Gary A. Parrett and J. I. Packer

Mere Christianity by C. S. Lewis

Simply Christian: Why Christianity Makes Sense by N. T. Wright

To Be a Christian: An Anglican Catechism,
edited by J. I. Packer and Joel Scandrett
Available online at https://anglicanchurch.net/catechism/.

"Concerning the Creeds," Q18–Q24

"Concerning Holy Scripture," Q25–Q35

"The Apostles' Creed, Article I," Q36–47

"The Apostles' Creed, Article II," Q48–83

"The Apostles' Creed, Article III," Q84–120

CHAPTER 3
PRAYER: THE BOOK OF COMMON PRAYER

*"Prayer should be the key of the day
and the lock of the night."*

—GEORGE HERBERT

IN EVERY AGE, men and women have talked with God in prayer. Prayer is one of God's main ways of communicating with His people. Through it, we build a relationship with God the Father, Jesus Christ the Son, and the Holy Spirit. Prayer brings us into direct communion with the Lord. Prayer is as essential to the spiritual life as air is to our lungs or water is to our cells. For that reason, there is nothing more universal than the practice of prayer. If you think about it, prayer is one of the practices Christians share in common around the world. There are people praying on every continent and every nation. One day in the not so distant future, the Bible tells us "every knee shall bow to me, and every tongue shall confess to God" (Rom. 14:11).

However, there are times when we simply don't have the words to express ourselves in prayer. When we don't know how to pray or when we need encouragement to pray, we look to the church. The prayers of fellow Christians can inspire and encourage us whenever we find ourselves at a loss for words, or when our desire to pray is not there. Many prayers and thanksgivings have been recorded and passed down, since the days of the Bible, to be used by others for mutual encouragement.

THE BOOK OF COMMON PRAYER

Until the Book of Common Prayer was published, the prayers and worship of the Church of England were in Latin, which the common person could not understand. This prayer book changed all of that by giving English-speaking people written prayers in their own language for the first time in history! Because it employed the language of the people, the Book of Common Prayer helped shape the devotional language of the English people by giving them a simplified prayer book that they could use anywhere, whether at church or at home.

"I became Anglican. Here's why...I started reading the BCP (a 1927 version), and it had me hooked, Bible readings, prayers, a liturgical calendar, I felt spiritually nourished by it. Second, I had to admit that being Anglican was also the best platform – certainly in Australia – to be Reformed and Evangelical. Third, as my interests became concurrently Reformed (in the sense recovering the apostolic gospel) and broadly Catholic (in the sense of recovering patristic sources for our theology) Anglicanism was the place to be since Anglicanism allows one to be both Protestant and Catholic." —MICHAEL F. BIRD[1]

Anglicanism employs a rich prayer book tradition that is unique among other Christian traditions. While other Reformation traditions developed confessional statements of faith, the Anglican tradition developed a prayer book, which is fundamentally pastoral and spiritual rather than theoretical. The Book of Common Prayer is one of Anglicanism's greatest contributions to the world. Commenting on its influence, author and theologian J. I. Packer reminded us, "Long before the age of fish and chips, the Book of Common Prayer was the great British invention, nurturing all sorts and conditions of Englishmen and holding the church together with remarkable effectiveness."²

Millions of people around the world have utilized the Book of Common Prayer, and it still influences Christians throughout the world today. It holds a place in history as one of the most beautiful prayer books ever composed. Second only to the King James Bible in religious readership, the Book of Common Prayer contains orders of services, ancient creeds, communal prayers, and a *lectionary* (a suggested reading plan for use throughout the year). It is a comprehensive service book, designed to provide (alongside the Bible itself), all the written text you need for public and private worship.

Its influence on English-speaking people cannot be overestimated. Over time, the Prayer Book influenced the development of the English language itself. According to historian Diarmaid MacCulloch, the Book of Common Prayer is "one of a handful of texts to have decided the future of a world language."³ Similarly, contemporary author Daniel Swift wrote about the essential influence of the Book of Common Prayer on the English people and their language in *Shakespeare's Common Prayers: The Book of Common Prayer and the Elizabethan Age*. Swift claimed, "The Book of Common Prayer is an extraordinary and too-often neglected work. . . . It is a skeleton beneath the skin of the best-known literary works of our or any time."⁴

Not only is the Book of Common Prayer widely used throughout the English-speaking world, but it also appears in many variations in churches in more than fifty different countries and in more than one hundred fifty different languages. Because of its widespread use, the words of the Prayer Book have become a familiar part of the English language, and, after the Bible, it is the most frequently cited book in the *Oxford Dictionary of Quotations*. Like the King James

Bible and the works of Shakespeare, many words and phrases from the Book of Common Prayer have entered popular culture, such as "ashes to ashes" and "till death do us part." Lutherans, Methodists, and Presbyterians alike have borrowed from the Book of Common Prayer, and its marriage and burial rites have found their way into other denominations and into English rhetoric. The Prayer Book has transformed both the Christian and cultural landscape ever since its inception in the 1500s.

COMMON PRAYER MEANS NEVER PRAYING ALONE

The use of the word "common" indicates the original purpose of the book. Related to our word "community," common doesn't mean "ordinary"; rather, it denotes something that is shared in common with others. Cranmer originally designed the book as a way to unite the people in worship through a liturgy where both the minister and the people prayed together. According to former Archbishop of Canterbury George Carey, "The fundamental purpose of celebrating common prayer is this: to help the church as a whole to pray together daily in a reflective and structured way."[5]

Prayer stands as a force that unites all of us as the church. By praying with the common prayer tradition, we find that we never really pray alone. Whether we are alone in a room or gathered with others in a small group, our prayers are united with believers both past and present. This is what theologian Scot McKnight described in *Praying with the Church* when he distinguished between praying *in* the church and *with* the church. Common prayer unites us with other believers around the world who are praying the same cycle of prayer throughout the day. The body of Christ has always been and will always be a praying church.

While the Prayer Book represents collective prayer, it also offers substance for the individual. Steve Wood, ACNA bishop of the Carolinas, grew up as a "cradle Anglican" in Ohio. Regarding the personal impact of the common prayer tradition, Bishop Wood said,

> Having grown up within the Anglican Tradition, I am quite familiar with the power and beauty of the Book of Common Prayer. Countless times I have found myself in personal and pastoral situations, both joyful and tragic, with the rhythms and vocabulary of ancient prayers on my lips. These words, these prayers drawn from the Scriptures themselves and prayed thousands of times, have shaped and molded my heart, my will, and my mind.[6]

USING THE BOOK OF COMMON PRAYER

If you are new to Anglicanism it can be a little intimidating to use the Book of Common Prayer. Is it a book for services of the church? Or is it a book for daily devotional? The answer is yes to both. To be honest, when first approaching the Prayer Book it can feel a little bit like trying to crack a code to a safe or putting together a puzzle. Where do you actually begin? This chapter is a short introduction to the Book of Common Prayer that can help you understand how to use it in worship and in your home.

It is important to remember that the purpose of the Book of Common Prayer is to put the prayers and liturgies into the hands of common people. It was originally designed to involve people in common worship and prayer, not to exclude them. Once you get used to the rhythms and cadences of the Book of Common Prayer, it becomes a part of your heart and soul. Prince Charles of Wales commented on how the words of the Book of Common Prayer have influenced his life: "As somebody who was brought up on that prayer book—day after day, year after year, Sunday after Sunday, school worship after school worship, evening prayer, communion, everything—those words do sink into your soul in some extraordinary way."[7]

The Book of Common Prayer can be divided into several sections.

- There is the daily office that has services for morning and evening prayer. The daily office can be used by individuals, families, or in worship with others.

- There are collects, which are prayers that are to be prayed throughout the seasons of the Christian Year.

- There are liturgies for Holy Baptism and Holy Communion as well as other services such as confirmation, Holy marriage, and burial for the dead.

- There is an ordinal with services for ordination of a bishop, priest, and deacon.

- There is a Psalter, which can be read daily throughout the year.

- There is a section that has the catechism, creeds, and Thirty-Nine Articles, which offer a concise summary of the essentials of the Christian faith.

- Finally, there is a lectionary, which is a systematic way of reading through the Scriptures throughout the year, either in private or public worship.

DISCOVERING THE DAILY OFFICE

We are creatures of habit. We all have rhythms, routines, and rituals that make up our daily lives. Most of us wake up in the morning and drink a cup of coffee, brush our teeth, and read the news. Or maybe we start the day off with a simple prayer and Bible reading. Routines and rituals are a good thing. They keep us on track and remind us of what matters most. Spiritually speaking, we need to have rhythms and routines to grow in our daily life in Christ.

One of the unique features central to Anglican prayer is a daily cycle of prayer called the Daily Office. For centuries, many Christians have employed this wonderful tool in their prayers. The Daily Office, or Divine Office, is based on the ancient practice of prescribed daily times of prayer. The name comes from the Latin *officium divinum*, meaning "divine office" or "divine duty." These services are accompanied by daily Scripture readings that include a reading from the Psalms, the Old Testament, and the New Testament.

The Daily Office originated from the Jewish practice of daily prayer in the Old Testament. God commanded the Israelite priests to offer sacrifices of animals in the morning and evening (see Exodus 29:38–39). As time went on, the Jewish people began to follow Torah readings, psalms, and hymns at fixed hours of the day. By the time of the Roman Empire, forum bells began the workday at 6:00 a.m., sounded mid-morning break at 9:00 a.m., the noon meal and siesta (or break) at 12:00 p.m., the recommencing of trade at 3:00 p.m., and the close of business at 6:00 p.m. Based on this routine, Christians began to order their prayer life around these times of the day.

By the second and third centuries, early church fathers such as Clement of Alexandria, Tertullian, and Origen wrote of the practice of the Daily Office. The prayers functioned for both individual and group settings, as in monasteries. Monasteries followed the fixed hours of prayer individually and corporately. As the monasteries continued to grow and spread throughout the Ancient Near East and into Europe, the monks took the practice with them.

Within this movement, Saint Benedict of Nursia established the most influential monastic rule in the sixth century for the community of monks at Monte Cassino. He established a "little rule for beginners" that brought together a balance of work and prayer. This included set times of prayer every three hours. This practice had such a great impact that when Pope Gregory the Great learned of Benedict's simple rule of prayer, he adopted it for the larger Roman Church. These hours of prayer continued through the Middle Ages and into the Reformation. While the monastic tradition employed a more frequent pattern of daily prayer, Thomas Cranmer condensed the Daily Office into Morning and Evening Prayer in his first Prayer Book, which many Christians still observe today.

Many people find that praying the Daily Office helps add a sense of regularity and balance to their prayer life. The Daily Office can help center you in the morning before you begin your busy day, and it can help calm you as you prepare for the hours of the night. You can use the Daily Office at your own pace. As you follow the Daily Office, allow yourself to slowly get into the rhythm of praying it in the morning and evening. You might find that, like millions of other Christians through the centuries, praying through the Daily Office is an enriching personal experience!

RECOVERING THE MEANING OF WORDS

In conclusion, the Book of Common Prayer has the power to help us recover the meaning of words. We live in a wordy world where words have virtually lost their meaning. This is due in part to an overabundance of words. You can't escape them because they are everywhere. Words in print. Words on signs. Words on billboards. Words on TV, computer, Facebook, Twitter, text messages: need I go on? The average American is bombarded with over 3,000 advertising messages a day! The Bible warns us, "In the multitude of words sin is not lacking" (Proverbs 10:19, NKJV).

Even though words are everywhere, we have become desensitized to their importance, especially when it comes to the spoken word. This has led to a breakdown in communication in our society. With the proliferation of words has come the rise of social media, like Facebook and Twitter, where you can have thousands of friends and followers. The result: talk is cheap, and relationships are superficial. People would rather text than talk. In spite of all of our communication and technological advances, people are lonelier and more depressed than ever before! The devaluing of words has also had a profound effect on how we pray and communicate with God. Many of our prayers are shallow, selfish, and lack any serious reflection upon the nature of God and the suffering of others. We don't need prayers that are longer or louder; we need ones that are more thoughtful and focused on God and His kingdom.

If history can teach us anything, it is the value and the importance of words. In particular, church history reminds us that words matter to God; therefore, they should matter to us. The Bible tells us, "In the beginning was the Word, and the Word was with God, and the Word was God" (John 1:1, ESV). God's spoken Word created the entire universe and everything in it. In the beginning God spoke His Word, and we have been speaking back to Him in prayer ever since. God has ordained words to be the means of communion with

Him. Prayer is our humble attempt to use words to respond to the God who spoke the world into existence.

The Book of Common Prayer is filled with prayers that are rich in theology and meaning. These prayers are literary masterpieces, which are bold, daring, poetic, and rich in meaning. When we open the Prayer Book, we find that it is full of wonderful, awe-inspiring prayers that have been recorded and passed on to inspire future generations. These prayers are scriptural and rich in theology, and although many of them are very old, their words are timeless and full of life and vitality. Dr. Richard Chartres, former bishop of London, comments on the literary beauty and power of the Book of Common Prayer: "The Book of Common Prayer which immerses us in the whole symphony of scripture; which takes us through the Psalms every month; which makes available in a digestible but noble way the treasury of ancient Christian devotion has a beauty which is ancient but also fresh."[8]

If you are looking for a Prayer Book, you should know that there are various versions of the Book of Common Prayer, ranging from the 1662 to more modern editions that have been produced around the world. In North America in recent decades, many of us cut our teeth on the 1979 Book of Common Prayer, the official Prayer Book of the Episcopal Church, having learned its cadences and memorized many of its prayers by heart. The previous Episcopalian Prayer Book, the 1928, is also still in use. I have recently begun using the new 2019 Book of Common Prayer, which is the official prayer book of the Anglican Church in North America. I have personally found it a wonderful modern version of the Book of Common Prayer, which builds upon earlier versions and stands in the great tradition of the 1662 BCP.

In closing, prayer is not something taught in a classroom; it must be learned through practice, repetition, and trial and error. Like an artist who spends years learning their craft, so a believer must commit him or herself to a life-long pursuit of learning how to pray. Just as a baby learns how to walk with tiny steps, or a child learns how to ride a bicycle with training wheels, we learn to pray by praying. There is no magic to it; we just pray. The Anglican Book of Common Prayer has helped millions of Christians learn how to pray by teaching them to pray through the timeless rhythms of life, by praying day by day, week by week, and year by year. New Testament scholar and Anglican Deacon Scot McKnight sums up the beauty and relevance of the Book of Common Prayer for a new generation in the following way. "*The Book of Common Prayer* affirms in me what I most believe about what Sunday worship and daily prayer ought to be: sacred words for sacred moments for a sacred people gathered for a sacred purpose."[9]

DISCUSSION QUESTIONS

1. After reading this chapter, how would you define "common prayer"?

2. In a world of informal communication, why would a historic prayer book tradition still be relevant?

3. As mentioned earlier, the Book of Common Prayer is one of the two most influential writings upon the English language. In what ways has it influenced the development of the English language?

4. As creatures of habit, how does the Daily Office help ground us in rhythms of prayer?

CLOSING PRAYER

Almighty and eternal God, so draw our hearts to you, so guide our minds, so fill our imaginations, so control our wills, that we may be wholly yours, utterly dedicated to you; and then use us, we pray, as you will, and always to your glory and the welfare of your people; through our Lord and Savior Jesus Christ. Amen.[10]

RECOMMENDED READING

Commentary on the American Prayer Book by Marion J. Hatchett

Prayer Book Spirituality: A Devotional Companion to the Book of Common Prayer Compiled from Classical Anglican Sources by J. R. Wright

Praying with the Church: Following Jesus, Daily, Hourly, Today by Scot McKnight

The Book of Common Prayer 1928, The Protestant Episcopal Church in the United States of America

The Book of Common Prayer 1979, The Episcopal Church

The Book of Common Prayer 2019, The Anglican Church in North America

The Book of Common Prayer: A Biography by Alan Jacobs

The Book of Common Prayer: The Texts of 1549, 1559, and 1662 edited by Brian Cummings

The Oxford Guide to the Book of Common Prayer: A Worldwide Survey by Charles Hefling and Cynthia Shattuck

To Be a Christian: An Anglican Catechism, edited by J. I. Packer and Joel Scandrett
Available online at https://anglicanchurch.net/catechism/.

"A Rule of Prayer: Scripture, Prayer, and Worship," Q224–Q255

Welcome to the Book of Common Prayer by Vicki K. Black

CHAPTER 4
LITURGY: ANGLICAN LITURGICAL WORSHIP

"The Liturgy declares the Gospel of God."
—Michael Ramsey

WORSHIP IS CENTRAL to who we are as Christians, and it is an essential aspect of what it means to be an Anglican. Worship is the act of giving all of ourselves back to God by giving Him respect, reverence, honor, and glory. The English word means "worth-ship" and carries the idea of worthiness. God is worthy of our highest praise and worship. God has called us to live "to the praise of his glory" (Eph. 1:12). We are here to glorify and know the God who created us. True worship of God begins in our hearts as we give adoration, glory, and praise to God, and then it manifests outwardly as we lift up our voices to God in prayer, praise, and song.

If you are new to Anglicanism, maybe you are thinking to yourself, "what is the difference between spontaneous worship and formal liturgy?" N.T. Wright offers a helpful contrast between the two, which may help the reader have a greater appreciation for the liturgy.

> There is nothing wrong with spontaneous worship, just as there's nothing wrong with two friends meeting by chance, grabbing a sandwich from a shop, and going off together for an impromptu picnic. But if the friends get to know one

another better and decide to meet more regularly, they might decide that, though they could indeed repeat the picnic from time to time, a better setting for their friendship, and a way of showing that friendship in action, might be to take thought over proper meals for one another and prepare thoroughly. In the same way, good Christian liturgy is friendship in action, love taking thought, the covenant relationship between God and his people not simply discovered and celebrated like the sudden meeting of friends, exciting and worthwhile though that is, but thought through and relished, planned and prepared—an ultimately better way for the relationship to grow and at the same time a way of demonstrating what the relationship is all about.[1]

When attending worship at an Anglican church, one of the first things you will recognize is the beauty of the liturgy. Anglicans share a common faith and liturgical form that unites us not only in our prayer, but also in our worship. In liturgical worship, Anglicans use communal words and symbols such as the Lord's Prayer, confession of sin, Scripture readings, and the Lord's Supper. These historic forms of liturgical worship and prayer help define the identity of Anglicans worldwide.

Concerning the richness of the Anglican liturgy, Anglican priest and founder of Methodism John Wesley once said, "There is no liturgy in the world, either in ancient or modern language, which breathes more of a solid, scriptural, rational piety than the Common Prayer of the Church of England."[2] The enduring legacy of historic Anglican liturgical worship is that it is scripturally based, doctrinally sound, and thoroughly gospel-centered.

LITURGY: ANGLICAN LITURGICAL WORSHIP

"Something kept me coming back. The preaching was expository and gospel-centered, but that was not the only reason I continued to attend. I was drawn to the singular effort of the whole service to direct our hearts to Jesus Christ. From the procession to the prayers, the songs to the sermon, the responsive liturgy to the Lord's Supper, not one part of the service was done unintentionally or irreverently. Everything pointed to Christ." —JONATHAN GROVES[3]

WHAT IS LITURGY?

If you are new to Anglicanism you may be wondering, what is liturgy? The English word "liturgy" comes from the Greek word *leitourgia*, which had originally been used as a secular term that referred to "public service" or a service rendered.[4] Over time the word liturgy began to take on a religious meaning. In the Greek Old Testament (Septuagint), the word *leitourgia* was used for the service rendered by the priests. In the New Testament, the word is used for the priestly services rendered by Zechariah, the father of John the Baptist (Luke 1:23) and it is used for the priestly ministry of Jesus Christ (Heb. 8:6). In Acts 13:2 it is used specifically for the worship of the church, and Paul used the term *liturgy* to refer to his voluntary service of gathering an offering for the poor (see 2 Corinthians 9:12). The term *liturgy* is not exclusively Christian, for it may also refer to the daily Muslim *salat* (prayers) and the Jewish *seder* (order).[5]

Today, the word liturgy generally refers to a set form of words, actions, and rituals done in worship. While the word "liturgy" often represents more formalized services in a high-church setting, every church has its own liturgy, no matter how unstructured its worship service may seem. The liturgy of the Anglican tradition functions to unite the body of believers in the essential work of the people: the worship of the One True God. The liturgy culminates in Holy Communion. In many ways, the liturgy provides essential vitamins that are missing in many contemporary evangelical worship services.

Are you new to the Anglican tradition and curious why Anglicans have a liturgical form of worship? There are several important aspects to understand about the value of Anglican liturgy. First, Anglican liturgy is God-centered versus man-centered. So much of contemporary Christian worship is "me-centered" and focuses on how "I" feel, feeding the ego. Liturgy frees us from worshiping ourselves and keeps the focus on the Triune God. With reading of Scripture, reciting Creeds, and confession, Anglican worship reminds us that real worship is about God, not us.

Second, Anglican liturgy is scriptural. It is estimated that nearly 80–90 percent of the historic liturgy is based on Scripture. Saturated with Scriptures from the Old and New Testament, the Word of God is the very foundation of the Book of Common Prayer, and thus Anglican worship. It is common to have three to four passages of Scripture read aloud during an Anglican worship service, not including the scriptural passages incorporated in the prayers.

Third, Anglican liturgy is communal and is meant to involve everyone in the worship service—it is *participatory*. Liturgy keeps us from being spectators and consumers by helping us engage in the worship of God with others. Liturgy, after all, is the "work of the *people*." The *antiphonal* (call and response) design of the worship services included in the Book of Common Prayer ensures that each person has the opportunity to participate in the liturgy.

Fourth, Anglican liturgy sanctifies time and space. The liturgy follows the Christian calendar, which calls us out of our secular time and orders the annual cycle of our lives around the life of Christ. Such rhythms and distinctions help to conform us to Christ within a worshiping context. The physical components of the liturgy (altar, candles, vestments, etc.) help to form sacred spaces of worship in our churches that allow us to enter the presence of God without distraction and with pure intentions. Anglicanism offers a rich multisensory worship experience that engages the whole person with touch, taste, smell, and feeling.

Fifth, Anglican liturgy unites us with the historic faith by inviting us to join the larger Christian story. In the liturgy, we participate in the same prayers, songs, and rhythms with Christians who have lived through the ages. Too often, contemporary Christians forget that there have been two thousand years of church history. This connection to the past offers a rich tradition of communal worship.

THE RHYTHM OF THE LITURGY

Every week, millions of Anglicans around the world retell the gospel story through liturgy. So, what is the structure of the Anglican liturgy? Like most ancient Christian liturgies, the Anglican liturgy a two-part journey: The liturgy of the Word and the liturgy of the Table.[6] The term "Word" refers to the place of Scripture reading, teaching, and preaching of the word of God in the worship service, and the "Table" aspect of this duo refers to the Eucharist or the Lord's Supper, which is an act remembering the death of Jesus Christ and anticipating His second coming by eating small pieces of bread or wafers and wine.[7] The Word and Table structure stands as a unique combination of prayer, scripture, preaching, and Holy Communion that forms and spiritually nourishes Christians through the liturgy.

The service of the Word begins in song and prayer, and then the reader(s) will read aloud as many as four passages of scripture. These readings usually include passages from the Old Testament, a Psalm, something from the Epistles, and a reading from the Gospels. The Psalm is usually recited aloud by the congregation while the others are read solely by the reader. After the scripture readings, a homilist will offer a sermon that is based on one of the readings appointed for the day. After the sermon, the congregation affirms their faith by reciting the Nicene Creed.

The Prayers of the People follows the Creed and is a time where the congregation prays together for the Church, the World, and those in need. The congregation then confesses their sins before God and one another. This is a corporate confession of sins of "what we have done and... what we have left undone,"[8] which is followed by a pronouncement of absolution. The absolution reminds the congregation that God is a God of grace, always ready to forgive us of our many sins. Having been forgiven, the congregation then greets one another with a sign of peace in a time that is called the passing of the peace. This concludes the services of the Word.

Without hesitation, the service moves from the Word portion to the Table portion where the congregation prepare themselves for Holy Communion. At the very heart of the Anglican liturgy is the Lord's Supper, which is commonly known as Holy Communion, or the Eucharist.[9] Since the beginning of the second century and possibly earlier the term "eucharist," which derives from a Greek word meaning "thanksgiving," has been used as a title for the service of holy communion.[10] The importance of the Lord's Table can be traced back to its vital role in the early life of the church.[11] The Eucharist (or "the thanksgiving") became the center of their worship together because it was an act of remembrance and a reminder of the future coming of Christ's final victory. The Eucharist offers congregants a way to respond tangibly to the message of God's Word.

The presider stands at the Communion Table, which has been set with a cup of wine and a plate of bread or wafers, and greets the congregation by saying, "The Lord be with you," and the congregation responds, "And with your spirit." The presider then prays the Eucharistic Prayer, which retells the story of our faith from Creation to the coming of Jesus Christ. The presider then blesses the bread and wine, and the congregation recites the Lord's Prayer together. Finally, the presider breaks the bread and offers it to the congregation as the "gifts of God for the People of God." The congregation then comes forward to the Table at the front of the worship space and partakes of the consecrated bread and the wine. After receiving Holy Communion, the congregation is blessed and sent back into the world on mission with the benediction and dismissal.

The balance of Word and Table is one of the riches that the Anglican tradition has preserved in its liturgical worship. As I mentioned in the introduction, I came from a low-church background that believed in the power of the Bible but had little interest in anything formally structured. I always felt like something was missing, and I longed for a deeper expression of the faith, which I found in the sacramental tradition. Let me explain. In seminary, I worked at a church that preached the Word faithfully each week but only celebrated Communion about once a year. Even then, the church did not approach the practice as a sacrament and only saw Communion as a memorial exercise—a vague memory of Christ's sacrifice. It felt like a last-minute add-on to the service with little, if any, spiritual significance. I sensed that there had to be more to celebrating the Lord's Supper than what I had experienced.

Then one day, I stumbled into a local Episcopal church in search of a service that had a sense of mystery and holiness without knowing exactly what I would encounter. With the help of the rector and three elderly ladies, I fumbled my way through the liturgy. To my surprise, I encountered the risen Christ at the Lord's Table that day. I will never forget the sacredness of the worship service, the reading of Scripture, the words of the prayers, and the burning sensation of the wine as I sipped from the chalice. It was in that little parish that I fell in love with the Anglican Eucharistic liturgy. The sacramental dimension of the Christian faith and the regular celebration of Communion became one of the strongest elements that drew me to Anglicanism from that day forward.

SEASONS OF THE CALENDAR

Each season brings its own unique rhythm, weather, traditions, and memories. Spring, summer, fall, and winter can be powerful reminders of the seasons and rhythms of the spiritual life. The Christian life has different seasons just like the seasons of nature. Each of these seasons reminds us of the multidimensional nature of the Christian life. In a similar way, Anglican liturgical worship revolves around the seasons of the church year. Each season has its own unique set of prayers, signs, symbols, and colors that are rich in meaning and theology.

> *"So why did I become an Anglican? I became an Anglican because the liturgy awakened in my soul the truth that lingered in the back of my consciousness and only came to full flowering on a Thursday night so many years ago. Anglicanism helped me recognize my need for Jesus. Having done that,*

LITURGY: ANGLICAN LITURGICAL WORSHIP

Anglicanism provided a means of meeting that need. It gave me the bread and wine. It gave me prayers, creeds, and a calendar of saints. People ask me what Anglicanism has to offer to black and brown people. We offer them Jesus and the church he created, nothing more, but in offering that we offer everything." —Esau McCaulley[12]

The early church began to observe the various themes of the gospel of Jesus Christ by celebrating different seasons of the Christian year. Churches in the Holy Land began developing liturgies to mark the days of Holy Week and Easter to commemorate the life and death of Jesus at specific holy sites. Pilgrims began to travel to Jerusalem to participate in these ceremonies and eventually brought the practices back with them to their countries of origin, and thus the practice of the Christian calendar spread.

Today, many different Christian traditions continue to play an important role in remembering the seasons of the Christian year. The church year involves an annual cycle of seasons including Advent, Epiphany, Lent, Easter, Pentecost, and Ordinary. Each season has its own unique set of prayers and themes that center on the gospel of Jesus Christ and prepare us for our journey of faith. What follows is a brief overview of the seasons of the church calendar and their meanings.

The season of Advent marks the beginning of the church year for Christians all over the world. It begins four weeks before Christmas Day, on the Sunday nearest November 30, and ends on Christmas Eve (December 24). During Advent, we prepare our hearts for the mystery both of Jesus' first coming in his Incarnation and birth by the Virgin Mary, and his second coming to judge the world at the end of the age.

The Christmas season immediately follows Advent and is also known as Christmastide. This season is made up of the traditional twelve days of Christmas and begins on December 25, lasting twelve days and ending with Epiphany on January 6. The Christmas season is short and made up of feast days in which we remember St. Stephen, the first martyr of the church, on December 26; the Feast of St. John the Evangelist on December 27; and Holy Innocents on December 28. While it is a joyful season, we also remember that there is pain and suffering in the world.

The season following Christmas is Epiphany, during which the church proclaims Jesus to the world as Son of God, Lord, and King. Many churches remember the coming of the wise men bringing gifts to the Christ child, whereby they reveal Jesus to the world as Lord and King. Jesus' Baptism in the Jordan and Transfiguration on Mt. Tabor are also celebrated. This season places a strong emphasis on the glorified human nature of Christ. Epiphany means "manifestation," "appearance," or "vision of God."

At Lent, we remember Christ's temptation, suffering, and death. Lent is a forty-day period beginning on Ash Wednesday that concludes the day before Easter. The climax of Lent is Holy Week, which immediately precedes Easter or Resurrection Sunday. Many Christian churches observe this as a time to commemorate and enact the last week of Jesus' life, His suffering (Passion), and His death through various observances and services of worship.

On Easter, we celebrate the glorious resurrection of Christ. The Easter season consists of the fifty days from Resurrection Sunday to Pentecost Sunday. Easter season celebrates the fact that Christ is risen! It recognizes God's ongoing work of establishing a new creation through the resurrection of Jesus Christ. It also celebrates the hope of that work being culminated in a new heaven and a new earth.

Pentecost, which literally means "fifty days after," falls exactly fifty days after Easter. At Pentecost, we celebrate the coming of the Holy Spirit into our lives and the church. The church uses this time to celebrate the reality that God, through the power of His Holy Spirit, continues to work in, through, and among His people.

The final season is commonly referred to as "Ordinary Time." The season's name comes, not from the notion of something ordinary, but from the word *ordinal*, which means, "counted time." Beginning on the first Sunday after Pentecost, this period focuses on specific themes of interest or importance to a local church.

COLLECTS OF THE CHURCH

Yet another aspect you will notice while attending an Anglican worship service is a prayer called a Collect. As the name suggests, the Book of Common Prayer is a book full of prayers for special seasons, days of the week, and prayers for families. Many of the prayers are called Collects and date as far back as the sixth century. A Collect is a prayer with a fixed form (address, petition, and conclusion) that is meant to be prayed communally. Often these are prayed by clergy leading the service, sometimes the congregation prays them aloud, and at other times we pray them quietly within our personal devotion time. Even when we pray these communal prayers privately, we are joining our hearts and minds with others who are praying the same prayer.

These prayers are not a substitute for personal or private prayer; rather, they are meant to enhance and deepen our personal prayer life. Author and theologian N. T. Wright lauded these prayers: "I love the weekly Collects in the Book of Common Prayer . . . Again and again they outshine, in their elegant but profound synthesis, more recent attempts to capture Christian truth and turn it into prayer."[13] When we pray these prayers, we connect to our Christian roots and stand with the great cloud of witnesses who have gone before us in the faith, as well as with millions of believers living today who are praying the same prayers. A beautiful and timeless example of a collect is traditionally known as the Collect for Purity, which is an ancient prayer that is prayed near the beginning of the Eucharist in most Anglican rites. A priest originally prayed it in preparation before the beginning of the Mass. Thomas Cranmer translated it from Latin into English, and it has become a central prayer in most Anglican liturgies around the world.

> Almighty God, to you all hearts are open, all desires known, and from you no secrets are hid: Cleanse the thoughts of our hearts by the inspiration of your Holy Spirit, that we may perfectly love you, and worthily magnify your holy Name; through Christ our Lord. Amen.[14]

WORSHIP POSTURE AND GESTURES

Last, the Anglican service represents a space for diverse individual expressions of worship. When attending an Anglican worship service, you will notice different people standing, sitting, kneeling, and making various gestures throughout the service. For worship, Anglicans sometimes use the adage, "Kneel for prayer, stand for praise, sit for instruction." This attitude recognizes that worshiping God involves our bodies as well as our minds and emotions. Through these gestures, Anglican worship engages the full spectrum of human senses by employing hearing, smelling, tasting, and touching.

LITURGY: ANGLICAN LITURGICAL WORSHIP

The following is a brief explanation of a few of the gestures you may encounter when you participate in Anglican worship, depending on the worship culture of the church you are attending. Bowing is a sign of reverence for and recognition of God's presence. For instance, people may bow when passing in front of the altar, when the cross passes by during a procession, or when the Gospel is read aloud. The second is the sign of the cross outlined on one's body. This motion symbolizes God's blessings on us through Christ's cross and expresses our trust in the work of Christ for our salvation. It is often made when the priest pronounces forgiveness of sin following corporate confession. The sign of the cross is made with the right hand, from forehead to chest or abdomen, then from left shoulder to right. The last gesture is that of briefly kneeling at certain points in the service. This act is called "genuflection," which is a traditional term that describes kneeling briefly on the right knee and returning upright. It is appropriate to genuflect in respect and honor of our Lord when approaching or passing an altar. Some parishioners genuflect as they leave their pew to partake in communion and also as they return.

However, there are many Anglican congregations that generally do not practice these forms of personal devotion. If you are mostly familiar with low-church (less formal) practices, these actions in Anglican worship service can seem a little intimidating at first. Please don't be intimidated by all the gestures. In Anglican worship, none of these gestures are mandatory. You are welcome to use the ones that aid your worship, but all of them are entirely optional. If you find certain ones helpful, then use them. "All may, none must, some should" is a good rule of thumb when we consider the various kinds of liturgical gestures in Anglican churches. At their core, they are designed to give glory to God and assist you in worshiping Him.

DISCUSSION QUESTIONS

1. How would you define the meaning of liturgical worship?

2. Do you agree with Todd Hunter's statement from the introduction that liturgical forms of worship are attractive to today's postmodern society? Explain why or why not.

3. How would you compare and contrast liturgical and contemporary forms of worship? What are some of the potential strengths and weaknesses of both?

4. How do the seasons of the Christian calendar help ground Christians in Christ-centered worship?

CLOSING PRAYER

O Almighty God, who pourest out on all who desire it the spirit of grace and of supplication: Deliver us, when we draw near to thee, from coldness of heart and wanderings of mind, that with steadfast thoughts and kindled affections we may worship thee in spirit and in truth; through Jesus Christ our Lord. Amen.[15]

RECOMMENDED READING

A Priest's Handbook: The Ceremonies of the Church
by Dennis Michno

Beyond Smells and Bells: The Wonder and Power of Christian Liturgy
by Mark Galli

Ceremonies of the Eucharist: A Guide to Celebration
by Howard E. Galley

LITURGY: ANGLICAN LITURGICAL WORSHIP

Liturgical Theology: The Church as Worshiping Community
by Simon Chan

The Meal Jesus Gave Us: Understanding Holy Communion
by N. T. Wright

The Shape of the Liturgy by Dom Gregory Dix

The Study of Liturgy, edited by Cheslyn Jones, Geoffrey Wainwright, Edward Yarnold SJ, and Paul Bradshaw

To Be a Christian: An Anglican Catechism,
edited by J. I. Packer and Joel Scandrett
Available online at https://anglicanchurch.net/catechism/

"Corporate Worship," Q244–251

CHAPTER 5
SACRAMENTS: BAPTISM AND EUCHARIST

> "In the bread and wine of the Eucharist, as in
> the sacrament of baptism, the past and future come
> to meet us in the present." —N.T. WRIGHT

TODAY, PEOPLE ARE HUNGRY for a faith that not only engages the mind but involves the senses of touch, taste, and smell. The historic church has asserted that we are cleansed with the water of baptism, fed with the bread and wine of Communion, and healed by the laying on of hands using anointing oil. We are taught by the read-aloud Word, as well as with the colors of the sanctuary that correspond with the seasons of the Christian year. All these elements function *together* in the sacramental practices of the church and engage us holistically.

While many churches have all but abandoned the regular celebration and practice of the sacraments, Anglicanism is a *sacramental* tradition that values the place of the sacraments in Christian worship. When I use the word "sacrament," I am referring to "an outward and visible sign of an inward and spiritual grace."[1] God has chosen ordinary earthly objects of water, bread, and wine as outward signs to signify the deep inner spiritual realities of the kingdom of God. Orthodox theologian Alexander Schmemann called this sacramental reality the "fourth dimension," which allows us to see the ultimate reality of life.[2] Theologian Robert Webber echoed Schmemann when he proclaimed, "A primary meaning of sacrament is that God works through his created order, through visible and tangible signs. For example, signs like bread, wine, oil, and laying on of hands are visible and tangible meeting points between God and people."[3]

The Church's outward signs reveal to us a deeper dimension of the Christian faith, one that is often lacking in much of contemporary Christianity. Our faith is not an isolated, one-dimensional experience that only impacts our hearts, souls, or minds. Instead, it must engage the whole of who we are, and the sacraments are an essential way in which God, through our faith, does this. The sacraments lead us into a faith that holistically transforms us—our hearts, souls, minds, and bodies.

"Our church plant's first major purchase was a chalice [...], because we were convinced that whatever God was bringing about, it would begin and end with His Incarnate Son celebrated in the Eucharist." —SHAWN MCCAIN[4]

The sacraments are intricately intertwined into the Anglican liturgy, each having its own service with a unique set of words and prayers that are ancient in their origin. There are two great sacraments of the gospel ordained and instituted by Jesus Christ Himself—Holy Baptism and Holy Communion.[5] Since the sacraments play an important role within the Anglican tradition, we need to take a moment to consider how they are a vital part of the Anglican worship service. As we shall see, these two sacraments are powerful and symbolic ways that, through participation in them, we are invited to enter into the redemptive story of God.

SACRAMENTS: BAPTISM AND EUCHARIST

WATER BAPTISM

In Anglican churches, you will regularly see infants, children, and adults being baptized with water as a part of the Sunday worship service. Baptism is essential to the Christian faith and occurs when a candidate is immersed in or has water poured or sprinkled on them in the name of the Father, the Son, and the Holy Spirit. This practice derives from the New Testament word *baptizo*, which means, "to dip into water." Baptism is a sacrament with multiple meanings and symbolizes that the believer has received forgiveness of sins and new life in Christ Jesus. While the outward and visible sign of baptism is water, the inward and spiritual grace set forth is "death to sin and new birth to righteousness, through union with Christ in his death and resurrection."[6] Commenting on the profound nature of baptism, Professor Michael Green stated, "The whole of the Christian life, in time and in eternity is, in a sense, encapsulated in baptism. The Christian life is a baptismal life, and it is all about dying and rising with Christ, in this world and hereafter."[7] Our baptism is communal and almost always happens in the context of worship, as it is our initiation into Christ's church, incorporating us into the body of Christ and giving us the Holy Spirit.

INFANT BAPTISM?

When I was first exploring Anglicanism, one of the major things I had to wrestle with was the practice of infant baptism. Over the years I've found out that I'm not alone. I am commonly asked the question, "Why do Anglicans baptize infants?" (For the record, Anglicans baptize infants, children, and adults alike.) From my experience, there are many people exploring Anglicanism who come from backgrounds that strongly hold to believer's baptism only. As a result, the historic practice of infant baptism makes it difficult for many to embrace Anglicanism.

It's worth noting what the ACNA Catechism has to say about this question:

> **129. WHY IS IT APPROPRIATE TO BAPTIZE INFANTS?**
> Because it is a sign of God's promise that they are embraced in the covenant community of Christ's Church. Those who in faith and repentance present infants to be baptized vow to raise them in the knowledge and fear of the Lord, with the expectation that they will one day profess full Christian faith as their own. *(Deuteronomy 6:6–9; Proverbs 22:6; Mark 2:3–5; Acts 2:39; 16:25–34)*[8]

Anglicans baptize infants to remain in continuity with the church's history and in response to Scripture's theology of covenant that dates back to Abraham. First, there is a historic precedent for infant baptism. The majority of all major Christian traditions have always baptized infants (Catholic, Orthodox, Anglican, Lutheran, Methodist, and Presbyterian, to name a few). Infant baptism has been the primary mode of baptism among Christians for more than two thousand years of church history. For me, the historic view of infant baptism was a hard case to argue against and, in fact, puts the burden of proof on those who have limited baptism to believers only, a phenomenon that only became common long after the sixteenth-century Reformation.

Second, the practice of infant baptism is rooted in the rich history of scriptural interpretation and the practices it promotes. Infant baptism traces its origins to the ritual of circumcision from the Old

Testament covenant. Following the example of Abraham (see Genesis 17:9–14 and 23–25), every male child born to an Israelite was to be circumcised eight days after he was born (see Leviticus 12:3) as a sign of God's covenant of grace.

As we get into the New Testament, we find that the earliest believers in Acts were baptizing everyone in their households and families (see Acts 16:33). Most of the theology for the practice of infant baptism comes from the writings of Paul. When Christ established a new covenant, baptism replaced circumcision as the sign that marked infants as children of the covenant. This is why Paul connects circumcision and baptism in Colossians 2:11–12: "In him also you were circumcised with a circumcision made without hands, by putting off the body of the flesh, by the circumcision of Christ, having been buried with him in baptism, in which you were also raised with him through faith in the powerful working of God, who raised him from the dead."

The third and most powerful reason for infant baptism relates to the second and grows out of Paul's teaching: a covenantal understanding of baptism makes a place for children in the covenant. Circumcision and baptism are both signs of God's covenant to His chosen people and precede an infant's ability to choose or speak for themselves. Whether adults or infants, we are passive recipients of God's grace. John Stott described baptism as a sacrament "of divine initiative, not of human activity. The clearest evidence of this in the case of baptism is that, in the New Testament, the candidate never baptizes himself, but always submits to being baptized by another. In his baptism, he is a passive recipient of something that is done to him."[9]

Like circumcision, baptism is not about a declaration of the child's faith in God; rather it is a sign of the covenant relationship between God and His chosen people. By being born into the family of God, a child is made a part of the covenant relationship long before they could articulate their own faith in God. God's covenant is the central principle at the heart of the Christian practice of infant baptism. On its own, apart from faith in Jesus Christ, baptism doesn't cause salvation (see Ephesians 2:8–9). But it is an effective sign of God's saving covenant grace. It is also important to note that while we do baptize infants, we consider it important that as these children grow, their parents encourage them to make a public declaration of their faith through confirmation.

HOLY EUCHARIST

Over the last few years, I have traveled to twelve countries on four continents, and I've learned that one of the most common human practices across all cultures is the sharing of meals. Eating is universal—no matter where you are from, you have to eat! Regardless of our cultural background, eating a meal with others represents a fundamental connection between human beings who want to grow in relationships. Few places are better for building relationships than the dinner table. Eating together naturally fosters community, friendship, and trust.

Patterned after this created reality, Christian liturgy leaves room for the power of a meal within the experience of worship. At the heart of the liturgy is a meal served at the Lord's Table, a meal known as the Lord's Supper, Communion, or the Eucharist. It's a meal shared in response to hearing the story of the plight of creation and God's offer of grace and redemption to humanity. Hearing the Word prepares us to come to the Lord's Supper, and the meal itself offers us a way to respond tangibly to the message of God's Word and the grace preached within it.

In the meal, the congregation comes forward to receive the grace of God through Communion with God and one another at the table. This is the church's act of remembering the death of Jesus Christ and anticipating his second coming by eating small pieces of bread (or wafers) and wine. The bread and wine are the "outward and visible sign" in Holy Communion, while the "inward gift signified" is "the Body and Blood of Christ, which are truly taken and received in the Lord's Supper by faith. *(Deuteronomy 8:1–20; Psalm 78:17–29; John 6:52–56; 1 Corinthians 10:1–4, 16–18)*."[10] As the ACNA Catechism elaborates, "As my body is nourished by the bread and wine, my soul is strengthened by the Body and Blood of Christ. I receive God's forgiveness, and I am renewed in the love and unity of the Body of Christ, the Church. *(1662 Catechism; Psalms 28:6–9; 104:14–15; Jeremiah 31:31–34; John 6:52–56; 17:22–24; Revelation 19:6–9)*."[11]

The importance of the Lord's Table can be traced back to its vital role in the early life of the church. The early church celebrated Communion every time they came together to worship, and in some cases, they practiced it daily.[12] In the Book of Acts, we can see that the life of the early church revolved around fellowship. At the heart of the Greek word for fellowship (*koinonia*) is the idea of participation. *Koinonia* is used to describe both the fellowship and actual participation in the Lord's Supper.[13] No single word in the English language fully captures the meaning of this Greek word. It's more than just a shared experience and nice conversation with other people. It is, at the deepest level, a spiritual connection in Christ, a supernatural bond provided by God's grace. This idea of fellowship is important for understanding what it means to live the sacramental life, and it is one of the reasons why young people are drawn to liturgy. The Christian life is rooted in living together in community, sharing life with one another and with Christ. We encounter the triune God in and through the regular worship of the church and in our participation in the Lord's Supper.

The early Christians viewed the Communion meals of *koinonia* as absolutely vital to their life as a church. In Acts 2:42, we read, "They devoted themselves to the apostles' teaching and to the fellowship, to the breaking of bread and to prayer." The "breaking of bread" (a reference to the Lord's Table) was a continual reminder of what Christ had done for them. It was also a reminder of God's ongoing presence and activity in the Church—past, present, and future. The Eucharist (or "the thanksgiving") became the center of their worship together because it was an act of remembrance and a reminder of the future coming of Christ's final victory. The Greek word for remembrance is *anamnesis*, which means a recollection of the past that enlivens and empowers the present. It is more than just a mental activity of individuals thinking about the past; it speaks to the ritual and verbal activity of communities.[14] For the early Christian community, the habits of remembrance and thanksgiving created a holistic approach to spirituality that celebrated God's holy presence in, with, and among them as they came together.

Throughout the ages, Holy Communion has typically been the climax of the liturgical worship gathering. At the Lord's Table, Christians are invited to partake of consecrated bread and wine. They are welcome to the table with the words, "the gifts of God for the people of God." As the congregation comes forward to the table at the front of the worship space and partakes of the bread and the wine, it embodies what heaven will be like—the union of God's people as one at Christ's table. At the table of the Lord, our differences no longer define us. Young, old, black, white, rich, and poor, are all welcome. The Lord's Table is the family table where all of God's children come and dine.

While a person only participates in baptism as a one-time initiatory rite, Anglican believers practice Holy Communion as a continuing rite. Week after week, millions of Anglicans around the world gather around the Lord's Table to partake of bread and wine during worship. Anglicans believe that we are continually fed and spiritually nourished as we share in the Lord's Supper. In the words of John Wesley, "As our bodies are strengthened by bread and wine, so are our souls by these tokens of the body and blood of Christ. This is the food of our souls: this gives strength to perform our duty and leads us on to perfection."[15] God's grace is given through the presence of the Holy Spirit as believers share in the memorial meal. Rowan Williams puts it beautifully, "When we gather as God's guests at God's table, the Church becomes what it is meant to be—a community of strangers who have become guests together and are listening together to the invitation of God."[16]

OTHER SACRAMENTAL RITES

Before we end this chapter, I would like to mention other sacramental practices that are commonly referred to as "sacramentals" or "sacraments of the Church." While Baptism and Holy Communion are two great sacraments of the gospel ordained and instituted by Jesus Christ Himself, other sacramental rites also developed in the life of the early church. These include confirmation, ordination, Holy Matrimony, absolution, and anointing of the sick. Each one possesses importance and functions as a means of conveying

God's grace to the lives of believers. The ACNA Catechism explains these sacramental rites by saying, "They are not commanded by Christ as necessary for salvation but arise from the practice of the apostles and the early church or are states of life blessed by God from creation. God clearly uses them as means of grace."[17] In confirmation, we are strengthened by the Spirit for mission; in ordination, ministers are called and ordained to serve the church; in Holy Matrimony, we are united in love and called to serve as the family of God; in absolution, we are forgiven and reconciled to right relationship with God and others; and in the anointing of the sick, we are witnesses of the hope and healing that is in Jesus Christ. Thanks be to God!

CONCLUSION

In conclusion, the sacraments also remind us that God is present with us in our every ordinary life. In fact, I think we often times miss God in the ordinary. God is truly our Immanuel, God with us, here and now. Rowan Williams reminds us that, "All places, all people, all things have about them an unexpected sacramental depth."[18] The sacraments remind us that faith is not just something we do once a week, but something we should incorporate into the daily routines of the home.

There is perhaps no better place to do this than the dinner table. Through the sharing of meals with one another, our homes become sacred places of hospitality and thanksgiving that echo the sacrament of the eucharistic celebration. Something as simple as a bowl of soup or a grilled cheese sandwich can become sacramental if it is made and received with love.

The Church's outward signs reveal to us a deeper dimension of the Christian faith, one that is often lacking in much of contemporary Christianity. Our faith is not an isolated, one-dimensional experience that only impacts our hearts, souls, or minds. Instead, it must engage the whole of who we are, and the sacraments are an essential way in which God, through our faith, does this. The Sacraments lead us into a faith that holistically transforms us—our hearts, souls, minds, and bodies.

DISCUSSION QUESTIONS

1. What is a sacrament?

2. How does the Anglican view of the sacraments differ from other non-sacramental traditions?

3. What do Anglicans believe about infant baptism, and how does that differ from the tradition you were raised in?

4. What do Anglicans believe about the Eucharist?

5. What are sacramentals, and how do they differ from the sacraments?

6. Is all of life sacramental? Explain.

CLOSING PRAYER

O Lord Jesus Christ, in this wonderful Sacrament you have given us a memorial of your passion: Grant us, we pray, so to venerate the sacred mysteries of your Body and Blood, that we may ever perceive within ourselves the fruit of your redemption; who live and reign with the Father and the Holy Spirit, one God, for ever and ever. Amen.[19]

RECOMMENDED READING

Case for Covenantal Infant Baptism by Gregg Strawbridge

Celebrating the Eucharist by Patrick Malloy

For the Life of the World: Sacraments and Orthodoxy by Alexander Schmemann

In the Breaking of Bread by Leander S. Harding

It Takes a Church to Baptize: What the Bible Says about Infant Baptism by Scot McKnight

Mystery of Baptism in the Anglican Tradition by Kenneth Stevenson

Sacramental Life: Spiritual Formation through the Book of Common Prayer by David deSilva

To Be a Christian: An Anglican Catechism, edited by J. I. Packer and Joel Scandrett
Available online at https://anglicanchurch.net/catechism/

"Concerning Sacraments," Q121–153

CHAPTER 6
SCRIPTURE: ANGLICANS AND THE BIBLE

"The Bible first, the Prayer Book next, and all other books and doings in subordination to both." —CHARLES SIMEON

ANGLICANS LOVE THE SCRIPTURES. In fact, when most people attend an Anglican church, the first thing they notice is the central role of the Bible. Each Sunday, there are usually four readings of Scripture: one from the Old Testament, one from the Psalms, one from the Epistles, and one from the Gospels. Commenting on this grand biblical heritage, bishop and scholar N. T. Wright says it well: "The reading of Scripture in the Anglican tradition is one of its great glories. Prayer Book (and Common Worship) Morning and Evening Prayer are basically showcases for scripture, which we read not simply to remind people of bits they may have forgotten but simply to declare the praises of God for his mighty acts."[1]

In this way, Anglicanism is firmly planted in the Reformation tradition of *Sola Scriptura* (by Scripture alone). With other Reformation traditions, Anglicans audaciously believe the Bible is not the work of mere men to be read like a novel or newspaper, but that it's actually the Word of the Living God. The Bible says, "All Scripture is given by inspiration of God" (2 Tim. 3:16 NKJV). Inspiration literally means *God-breathed*. So, if you believe the Bible is actually God's inspired Word, then the implications are absolutely astounding and a whole new world of possibilities begins to open up to you.

> *"When I first began attending an Anglican church, I quickly noticed how much Scripture is read aloud in worship. Growing up in an evangelical church, I had always been told to read Scripture every day, alone with God. This is a wonderful practice. But it was in the Anglican church that I learned the importance of the public reading of Scripture."*—GREG GOEBEL

While the traditional documents reviewed in the previous chapter reveal much of the Anglican belief system, Anglicans ultimately turn to the Bible as the source of all beliefs. Time and time again, Christians throughout the ages have searched God's Word to find strength and encouragement for life's greatest challenges. Although the Bible isn't a magical answer book, it is the place where one learns about God's plan and purposes. The Bible offers a foundation of faith so that we can find answers to many of life's toughest questions within the larger story it is telling.

ANGLICANS AND THE SCRIPTURES

One can see this love of Scripture by looking to history and seeing the way Anglicans have produced a number of the earliest translations of the Bible into English. A few notable Anglicans have helped in translating Scripture. In the 1380s, John Wycliffe produced the first English translation of the New Testament from the Latin Vulgate. Wycliffe has been known as the "Morning Star of the Reformation" because of his desire to translate the Bible into the language of the common people.

During 1525–1526, William Tyndale wrote a translation of the

New Testament from the original Greek. William Tyndale is called the father of the English Bible. He attended Oxford and Cambridge and eventually left the university world to translate the English Bible from the original Hebrew and Greek. Unfortunately, the church was opposed to his attempts at translating the Bible into the language of the English people and he was forced to go into hiding. He became known as "God's outlaw." Despite persecution and attempts on his life, Tyndale eventually succeeded in translating the entire New Testament and some of the Old Testament into English. In 1535, he was betrayed by a friend and arrested. He paid for his work with his life and was strangled and burned at the stake near Brussels. However, in the end, Tyndale was victorious because his translation became the basis for English translations of the Bible since that time.

In 1604, King James I of England authorized a new English translation of the Bible that would be read by Christians across England. He commissioned a team of biblical scholars to translate the Bible into English. It was finished in 1611, and quickly became the standard for English-speaking Protestants around the world. It became known as the King James Version of the Bible. Its poetic language and lyrical rhythm have had a profound influence on the development of the English language and literature for over 400 years. The King James Bible continues to be read by millions of Christians around the world.

PRAYER AND THE BIBLE

Anglicans believe that prayer and Bible study are inseparably linked. Scripture should always be read in the context of prayer because prayer is the medium that brings us into contact with the same Holy Spirit who inspired the authors of the Bible. As we read the Scriptures, the Spirit applies the truths of the Word to our hearts. Prayer is the necessary means whereby we understand the Word of God. Without the assistance of the Holy Spirit in prayer, our Bible study will be in vain.

As we discussed in previous chapters, Anglicanism arose out of the Reformation, and from its inception proclaimed that the "Holy Scriptures containeth all things necessary to salvation."[2] Strongly influenced by Reformation thinkers of his day, Thomas Cranmer wholeheartedly believed in the importance of spending time in the Scriptures daily. This explains why the Word of God functions as the very foundation of the Book of Common Prayer, which is saturated with Scriptures from the Old and New Testament. Cranmer once said, "The people (by daily hearing of holy Scripture read in the church) should continually profit more and more in the knowledge of God and be the more inflamed with the love of his true religion."[3]

For Cranmer, Scripture and prayer hold to one another through an intricate connection. In his mind, these pillars of the faith should not be separated. Cranmer's vision for the Daily Office was a matrix of prayer and Scripture woven together, exposing the reader to the presence of the Living Word. Cranmer's collect for the second Sunday of Advent shows his intimate love for the Scriptures:

> Blessed Lord, who caused all Holy Scriptures to be written for our learning: Grant us so to hear them, read, mark, learn, and inwardly digest them, that by patience and the comfort of your holy Word we may embrace and ever hold fast the blessed hope of everlasting life, which you have given us in our Savior Jesus Christ; who lives and reigns with you and the Holy Spirit, one God, for ever and ever. Amen.[4]

Thomas Cranmer's vision for Anglicanism included reading Scripture daily throughout the year. He restored the ancient practice of reading through the entire Bible in daily prayer. His greatest desire was to put the Bible and prayer in the hands of ordinary people so that they would be in a place where the God of the Bible could transform their hearts and lives. This is why Cranmer devised a Bible reading plan (*lectionary*) through which everyone could hear the Scriptures on a regular basis. Bishop John Howe said of Cranmer's scriptural legacy, "In a stroke, he made the Church of England the greatest Bible-reading church in the world. Nowhere else is the Bible read so regularly, so comprehensively, and at such length as in the public worship of the Anglican Communion."[5]

The enduring legacy of the Book of Common Prayer owes a debt to the book's scriptural basis and doctrinal accuracy. The Prayer Book contains the entire book of Psalms and also a reading plan for the entire Bible; thus, biblical references and doctrinal themes pervade its words and prayers. Dr. John Sentamu, archbishop of York, reminded us, "The Prayer Book places the Bible at the heart of the church's worship and on the lips of the people. It teaches the grace and mercy of God, and it preaches Jesus as a living Savior, not a dead master of a bygone age."[6]

THE LECTIONARY

Reading the Bible can be a little overwhelming at first because of its sheer size and the extent of its different doctrines, characters, stories, and themes. But there is good news: we don't have to be systematic theologians to read and understand God's Word. Reading the Bible is more like a marathon than a sprint, so I recommend that you start small and finish big. It will take a lifetime to study the entire

Bible, and even then, we will never know all there is to know about it. To help with this daunting task, the Anglican tradition has a historic and systematic way that every Christian can read and hear the Scriptures throughout the Christian year. Here are several things that we can learn about reading the Bible from Cranmer's preface to the 1549 Book of Common Prayer.

- The Bible should be read by everyone. In the spirit of the Reformation, Cranmer wanted every man, woman, boy, and girl to have access to the Word of God in their own language.

- The Bible should be read every day. Cranmer wanted to Christians to be exposed to the Word of God daily through morning and evening prayer.

- The Bible should be read through in a year. Cranmer devised a Bible reading plan that would allow people to hear the Bible read through in a year.

- The Bible should be read privately and publicly in worship. The uniqueness of Cranmer's common prayer is that it was meant to facilitate both private and public reading of Scripture.

As mentioned above, the Book of Common Prayer contains a systematic Bible reading plan called a "lectionary." A lectionary is simply a list of Bible passages for personal reading and study, or for preaching in services of worship. The lectionary readings from the Book of Common Prayer are used for daily services of worship and for Morning and Evening Prayer. In Cranmer's first Prayer Book of 1549, the lectionary appeared as a guide for twelve months, January to December, and provided Old Testament and New Testament lessons for every day of the year. Cranmer intended the Scriptures to be read at Morning and Evening Prayer so that they would become ingrained into the daily rhythms of peoples' lives.

Since that time, there have been many versions of the daily lectionary. Some lectionaries go through the Bible in a year, while others follow a two or three-year cycle, often following the seasons of the Church calendar. It is also worth noting that there are Daily Office lectionaries, which tell you what Bible passages to read during Morning and Evening Prayer, and Sunday and Holy Day lectionaries, which tell you what to read during public worship services (usually celebrated with Holy Communion). In recent years, there has been a move toward uniformity among the various lectionaries, such as the Revised Common Lectionary. Regardless of which lectionary or Bible-reading plan you follow, there is nothing more important than a regular reading of the Scriptures.

THE ORIGINAL PRAYER BOOK: THE PSALMS
One of the best ways to begin reading Scripture daily is by starting with the book of Psalms, which is also known as the Psalter. There are exactly one hundred fifty psalms, which are songs of worship that explore a wide range of diverse subject matter related to the life of God's people. Topics such as war, peace, repentance, forgiveness, joy, happiness, worship, praise, and prayer can be found within the pages of the Psalms. The Psalms have provided comfort and guidance for thousands of weary pilgrims who share in the journey of life. The Psalms remind us that we are not alone in our pilgrimage, but that God is with us.

The Psalms have been the prayer book for God's people since

before the time of Christ. Author Eugene Peterson said, "The Psalms were the prayer book of Israel; they were the prayer book of Jesus; they are the prayer book of the church."[7] They have been a part of the daily rhythm of the church's Bible reading since its earliest days, and they continue to be an important part of the church's private and corporate prayer. It could be said that the reason for the popularity of the Psalms is because they explore a wide range of human emotions and experiences: from delight to despair. In a way, the Psalms express feelings common to all people.

Thomas Cranmer had a profound love and admiration for the Psalms which he inherited from ancient and medieval Christian practice of praying through the Psalms. In fact, he instituted a thirty-day cycle of reading the Psalms, which is still printed in the Psalter of the Book of Common Prayer. By following his cycle of daily readings, you can read through all the Psalms on a monthly basis, repeating them twelve times a year. After a while, you will become intimately acquainted with the Psalms in such a powerful way that they will always be with you no matter where you are or what you are going through.

The Book of Common Prayer contains a thirty-day cycle for reading through the book of Psalms. In the months that are shorter than thirty days, you can read extra Psalms on the last few days of the month. Likewise, in months with thirty-one days, you can simply choose additional Psalm readings. Once you have finished the thirty-day cycle, you can start the journey through the Psalms again on the first day of the next month. (Note that the BCP 2019 also contains a sixty-day cycle for reading through the Psalms, and the BCP 1979 contains a seven-week cycle.)

The Lord will meet with you as you prayerfully read through the book of Psalms each month. Cranmer poetically said, "In the Scriptures be the fat pastures of the soul."[8] This means that the Scriptures are the very place where we encounter the Lord and where He feeds us with His daily bread. It was Cranmer's deep hope that, in this way, all Anglicans would hear, read, mark, learn, and inwardly digest the Scriptures. Just as Moses encountered God in the burning bush, we also come face to face with God through the Scriptures. A. W. Tozer reminded us: "The Bible is not an end in itself, but a means to bring men to an intimate and satisfying knowledge of God, that they may enter into Him, that they may delight in His Presence, may taste and know the inner sweetness of the very God Himself in the core and center of their hearts."[9]

DISCUSSION QUESTIONS

1. How have Anglicans demonstrated their love and dedication to the Scriptures throughout the centuries?

2. How does the Anglican tradition stand in line with the Protestant Reformation's emphasis on the priority of Scripture?

3. In what ways has the Bible played a central role in Anglican worship and prayer?

4. How and why is the Bible essential to the spiritual life of all Christians, regardless of their background or tradition?

CLOSING PRAYER

Blessed Lord, who caused all Holy Scriptures to be written for our learning: Grant us so to hear them, read, mark, learn, and inwardly digest them, that by patience and the comfort of your holy Word we may embrace and ever hold fast the blessed hope of everlasting life, which you have given us in our Savior Jesus Christ; who lives and reigns with you and the Holy Spirit, one God, for ever and ever. Amen.[10]

RECOMMENDED READING
Biblical Interpretation: Past & Present by Gerald Bray

New Testament History by F. F. Bruce

Scripture and the Authority of God: How to Read the Bible Today by N. T. Wright

The Blue Parakeet: Rethinking How You Read the Bible by Scot McKnight

To Be a Christian: An Anglican Catechism, edited by J. I. Packer and Joel Scandrett
Available online at https://anglicanchurch.net/catechism/

  "Concerning Holy Scripture," Q25–Q35

What Saint Paul Really Said: Was Paul of Tarsus the Real Founder of Christianity? by N. T. Wright

CHAPTER 7
ORDER: ANGLICAN HOLY ORDERS AND STRUCTURE

> "The impact of the gospel has led on to the structure of the church."
> —MICHAEL RAMSEY

THE CHURCH EXISTS as the spiritual and living body of Christ. In 1 Corinthians 12:12–27, Paul portrays the corporate church like that of a human body. In Paul's metaphor, every part has an important role to play in the whole. The rest of the New Testament agrees with Paul's representation of the church as an organic whole, made one in Christ.. Nowhere in the New Testament do we find the word "church" referring to a building. In its earliest expression, the church stood for a group of individuals who had come together in the name of Jesus Christ. The Greek word for church is *ecclesia*, which literally means "the called-out ones." You may ask, called out from what? The answer to this question is simple: the world. At the deepest level, the church is made up of individuals who are called out of a disordered world by God to live differently and be a part of God's order, His family. Accordingly, people of all ages in all times who are true believers and followers of Christ have made up the church.

Interestingly enough, many dictionaries describe church as "a place of public worship." Over time, the concept of church has shifted from being a body to becoming a building. People have gotten it backward. Because of this shift, followers of Jesus must get back to an organic understanding of what it means to be the church. Like all healthy organisms, the church requires numerous systems and structures that work together to fulfill its intended purpose and ensure its overall health. Just as the physical body must have an organic structure to hold it together in order to enable growth and development, so the body of Christ must have an organic structure that can do the same. In this way, Anglicanism embodies an organic and ordered faith that is locally, nationally, and globally connected as it embraces the historic threefold order of ordained ministry.

HOLY ORDERS

The phrase "holy orders" refers to the threefold order of ordained ministry that emerged early in the life of the church and continues today. The offices of bishop, priest, and deacon constitute this threefold order. The "holy" aspect of holy orders represents how these offices have been set apart for some purpose, while the word "order" comes from the Latin word *ordo* and designates an established pattern for ordination.

Harkening back to the theme of the body, Jesus Christ is the Head of the church. He is the Alpha and Omega, the beginning and the end of the church. Jesus loves the church and gave Himself up as a sacrifice for her (see Ephesians 5:25), so that He could build her from the ground up (see Matthew 16:18). Jesus is the very foundation of the church, and without Him, the church cannot exist. Not only is He the foundation, but He is also the one who adds to the church. Luke tells us, "The Lord added to their number day by day those who were being saved" (Acts 2:47). Therefore, as followers of Christ, the church gathers together to perpetuate the message of the gospel in all places and for all ages.

ORDER: ANGLICAN HOLY ORDERS AND STRUCTURE

> *"I'll never forget the first time I was invited to a Clergy Day luncheon in our Diocese. I got to see a team of ministers working and praying together like never before! I got to sit under the godly leadership of a bishop with decades of experience in ministry. It was thrilling and humbling. Being within and under the godly three-fold ordering of bishops, priests, and deacons has given me the chance to see catholicity alive. This is how it's supposed to look!* —Justin Clemente[1]

Early in His ministry, Jesus Christ called a handful of men to follow Him and be His disciples, and they came to be known as the twelve apostles. We see this in the Gospel of Mark: "He appointed twelve (whom he also named apostles) so that they might be with him and he might send them out to preach and to have authority to cast out demons" (Mark 3:14–15). As the apostles continued Christ's mission, they needed to ordain new converts to join them in leading the church. This ordination practice was characterized by the apostles laying their hands on individuals called to ordained ministry (see Acts 6:1–7).

By the beginning of the second century, the terms "bishop," "priest," and "deacon" had achieved widespread acceptance in forms that signified offices virtually identical to those used by Anglicans today. The early church fathers recognized all three offices and regarded them as essential to the church's structure. The letters of Ignatius, bishop of Antioch, are especially significant in defending the development of the threefold order of ordained ministry. In his *Letter to the Magnesians,* Ignatius wrote, "Take care to do all things in harmony with God, with the bishop presiding in the place of God, and with the presbyters in the place of the council of the apostles, and with the deacons, who are most dear to me, entrusted with the business of Jesus Christ, who was with the Father from the beginning and is at last made manifest."[2]

As with other Christian traditions, Anglicanism holds to the historic threefold order of the ordained ministry of bishops, priests, and deacons. While all Anglicans believe that bishops are the successors of the apostles, they differ in how they understand that succession. For many Anglicans, this is more spiritual than historical succession—bishops are "apostolic" because they teach the apostolic faith and act as modern day apostles for the Church. However, some Anglicans also believe that a bishop's authority must come through the laying on of hands by other bishops who trace their ordination back to the apostles and ultimately to Christ. It's worth noting that this "chain" is meant to help ensure the continuity of apostolic teaching. From the time of Augustine of Canterbury to today, Anglican bishops can trace their ordination back in an unbroken line. In the ordination process, only bishops may ordain new candidates into the ministry of holy orders.

The various versions of the Book of Common Prayer provide an ordinal, which is a service book with rites for ordination of bishops, priests, and deacons. The preface of the Ordinal for the Anglican Church in North America states,

> The Holy Scriptures and ancient authors teach that, from the Apostles' time, these three orders of ministry have existed in Christ's Church: Bishops, Priests, and Deacons. From the earliest days of the Church, these offices were always held in such reverent estimation that no one might presume to execute any of them without being first called, tried, examined, and ascertained to have such qualities as are requisite.[3]

ORDER: ANGLICAN HOLY ORDERS AND STRUCTURE

BISHOP

The bishop fulfills his role by serving as the chief pastor of a local diocese of churches. The bishop stands as the guardian and teacher of the faith, fosters unity, executes discipline when needed, and proclaims the Word of God (see Titus 1:7–9; 1 Timothy 3:1–7; Acts 20:28). Bishop comes from the New Testament Greek word *epískopos*, which means "overseer" or "guardian." This is where we get our modern word *episcopal*, which refers to the spiritual oversight of a bishop. In order to become a bishop, a person must already be a priest.

The role of the bishop also includes ordaining others to continue Christ's ministry on earth. Within Anglicanism, three bishops are normally required for ordaining and consecrating someone to the episcopate, while one bishop is sufficient for ordaining priests and deacons. Anglican bishops are often identified by wearing purple clergy shirts and usually wear a pectoral cross and a bishop's ring as a sign of their office. Purple is traditionally the color of royalty and symbolizes the bishop's connection to Christ. On more formal occasions, bishops carry a large staff called a crosier as the sign of their shepherding ministry, a hat called a mitre, and a liturgical vestment called a cope.

Why do Anglicans have bishops? Two words: submission and support. The idea of submission can seem contrary to the radically independent American spirit, but a growing number of people are looking for the support that comes from having a bishop in their life. On a personal level, having a bishop is one of the things that I appreciate most about Anglicanism. There are a lot of reasons I love being Anglican, but having a bishop is one of them. My bishop Steve Wood first ordained me as a deacon and then as a priest. Over the years he has been a mentor and has supported and encouraged me in so many ways. Before becoming an Anglican, I was doing ministry on my own, but now I have the support of a bishop and a rich tradition that gives me a foundation for my faith.

PRIEST

The ministry of a priest is to share with the bishop in the overseeing of the church by serving as a pastor and teacher to the people. The priest also preaches and teaches the Word of God and is authorized to administer the sacraments in the local church. The priest pronounces the absolution and blessing in God's name. Priests function in the role of "elders" as described in the New Testament (see Titus 1:5ff; 1 Peter 5:1ff). Etymologically, the English word "priest" comes from the New Testament Greek word for "elder," *presbýteros*, and not from the word for (sacrificial) "priest," *hiereus*. Unlike Catholic priests who must remain celibate throughout their life, Anglican clergy are allowed to marry.

Anglican priests sometimes serve as the rector/pastor of local churches or in a variety of other ministry positions such as hospital chaplaincy. Priests are sometimes called "Father" or "Reverend," which refers to their pastoral and spiritual oversight of others. They also typically wear clergy shirts, which are often black and have a detachable collar or tab to distinguish them as members of the clergy.

DEACON

Deacons assist bishops and priests in the proclamation of the gospel and the administration of the sacraments. Deacons are the lead servants in the community of faith. The apostles in Acts 6 began the tradition of ordaining deacons for serving the church. The work of deacons facilitates the ministry of the body and frees up the priests so that they may focus more heavily upon the proclamation of the Word and performing the sacraments. Deacons become the hands and feet of our church, the body of Christ (see 1 Corinthians 12:27).

The basic meaning of the Greek word "deacon" (*diákonos*) suggests the role of a servant (see John 2:5; Romans 15:8; Matthew 20:26; Acts 11:29), especially in regard to providing practical help with respect to the basic necessities of life (see Matthew 4:11, 8:15, 27:55; Luke 10:40; Romans 15:25). Although deacons may assist with the sacraments and can baptize when given permission by their bishop, only bishops and priests can preside over the Eucharist and consecrate the elements. The deacon is also a servant of those in need (see Acts 6:1–6; 1 Timothy 3:8–13). Deacons may either be "transitional," meaning they plan to eventually become a priest, or they may remain a lifelong "vocational" deacon as a servant of the church. Finally, it is important to note that bishops and priests always remain deacons and servants of the church throughout their ministry.

A WORD ON WOMEN'S ORDINATION

It's important to note that the rapid growth of Anglicanism would not have been possible without the tireless work and self-sacrifice of female leaders. If we look throughout the centuries, we will find that women contributed to the ministry of the church in significant ways, even though their involvement has rarely been free from controversy.

While there is not enough room here to engage the entire debate on the ordination of women, I would like to offer a quick overview of the issue in the Anglican Communion. Florence Li Tim-Oi was the first woman to be ordained to the priesthood, and she was ordained on January 25, 1944 by Ronald Hall, bishop of Victoria, Hong Kong. To avoid controversy, she resigned her license to administer the sacraments after the end of the Second Sino-Japanese

War. Then, at a Synod in 1971, the Province of Hong Kong and Macao became the first Anglican province to officially ordain women to the priesthood, at which time Jane Hwang and Joyce Bennett were ordained to the priesthood and Li Tim-Oi was officially recognized again as a priest.

Since that time, the ordination of women in the Anglican Communion has been increasingly common throughout the Provinces and Dioceses. In the United States, Barbara Harris was the first woman to be consecrated as a bishop by the Episcopal Church in February 1989. Twenty-six years later, the Church of England followed and consecrated Libby Lane at York Minster on January 26, 2015.

Today, there is widespread diversity and debate over the issue of women's ordination.[4] Although debates on women in ministry within Protestant evangelicalism often focus on preaching and teaching, Anglican debates on women's ordination also involve matters of church order and sacramental ministry. One example of diversity over the issue of women's ordination comes from the Anglican Church in North America, which calls the differing views on women's ordination "two integrities." Some dioceses within the ACNA ordain women, while others do not. In an official statement on women's ordination, the ACNA states:

> At the inception of the Anglican Church in North America, the lead bishops unanimously agreed to work together for the good of the Kingdom. As part of this consensus, it was understood that there were differing understandings regarding the ordination of women to Holy Orders, but there existed a mutual love and respect for one another and a desire to

move forward for the good of the Church. This commitment was deeply embedded in the Constitution and Canons overwhelmingly adopted by the Inaugural Assembly (2009).[5]

When it comes to the ordination of women, most Anglicans agree to disagree and choose to walk together in love despite disagreements. Although several provinces and certain dioceses only ordain men, the majority of Anglican provinces ordain women to at least one holy order. Some provinces ordain women to bishop, priest, and deacon; others ordain women as deacons and priests but not as bishops; and still others only ordain women as deacons. There are also Anglicans who "set apart" women as deaconesses, but do not consider this an ordained holy order. Regardless of what your views are on women's ordination, I believe that Christians should walk together in love despite differences of opinion. As an advocate for women's ordination myself, I think this provides for a healthy balance where people on both sides of the argument can be a part of the same church and serve a common mission.

LAY LEADERSHIP

There is a misconception that Anglican ministry belongs completely to the ordained clergy; nothing could be further from the truth. Over the centuries many of the most important Anglicans have not been members of the ordained clergy at all but have been everyday lay persons. Anglicanism has a rich tradition and heritage of lay leadership. In fact, throughout the ages, one of the most important members of the Church of England has been a lay person: the reigning King or Queen of the time. But the reach of significant Anglican lay leadership extends far beyond royalty.

One of the most popular and significant Christians of the 20th century was C.S. Lewis. An internationally known British author, scholar, lay theologian, and professor, Lewis wrote many influential treatises and novels while also teaching at prestigious schools such as Cambridge and Oxford. In his day, Lewis wrote more than thirty books, including poetry, children's books, and numerous books on Christianity. Lewis reminds us that we need both ordained and lay people to serve in the church today. Anglicanism has a rich history and heritage of lay people who have helped shaped the world in which we live in significant ways.

THE LOCAL CHURCH

For Anglicans around the world, the local church stands as the primary place of belonging and living out the Christian faith. According to the constitution and canons of the Anglican Church in North America, "The fundamental agency of the mission of the church to extend the Kingdom of God is the local congregation. The chief agents of this mission are the people of God."[6] By coming together as a congregation, the people of the local church form an extension of the global body of Christ. But how does this happen? Article XIX of the Thirty-Nine Articles of Religion reveals how this becomes a reality: "[A congregation is] a gathering where the pure Word of God is preached and the sacraments are duly administered according to Christ's ordinance."[7] For Anglicans, the local church is where we grow in our faith together by hearing the Word of God preached, by partaking in the sacraments, and by being sent out in mission.

While the elements of Word and sacrament form the foundation of practice, local Anglican churches (often called "parishes") fit within the organizational structure of the larger Anglican church by organizing and connecting to a diocese and submitting themselves under the oversight of a bishop. Local Anglican churches are presided over by a priest (occasionally, and usually temporarily, by a deacon) who provides the congregation with spiritual and sacramental leadership. In addition, each local church is governed by a local board known as the vestry, which is a group of women and men who are elected by the congregation to handle the temporal everyday affairs of the church. From the smallest parish to the largest diocese, the Anglican Communion represents a diverse but unified body of believers connected by a common faith and tradition.

DIOCESE

In addition to the role of ordained ministry and the local church, Anglicans are a part of a larger structure that holds them together in geographic regions around the world. Each Anglican congregation holds a place of membership within a local diocese. The word "diocese" comes from the time of the Roman Empire, which was divided into twelve different administrative and governmental dioceses. As the church grew, so did the need to create an organizational structure. The early church borrowed from the Roman governmental structure to organize local clusters of churches in a region.

Today, a diocese is a cluster of churches in a distinct geographic region under the leadership of a bishop. Some dioceses, like the Anglican Diocese of the Carolinas, are made up of churches in a broad area (in this case, throughout North and South Carolina), while others comprise a larger number of churches within a city, like the Diocese of London. At times, there are also non-geographic dioceses that are more affinity-based in nature, such as Churches for the Sake of Others (C4SO), led by Bishop Todd Hunter who oversees churches across the United States.

PROVINCES

Each diocese is a part of a national province led by an archbishop, the most senior bishop of a province. Another term for an archbishop who is over a national province is a "Primate." Like a diocese, the word "province" comes from the ancient Roman word "provincial," which was the major territorial and administrative unit of the Roman Empire's territories outside of Italy. A province is a larger geographic grouping of dioceses usually representing a nation, like the Anglican Church of Uganda. The minimum to constitute a province is usually four dioceses. Some provinces have distinct boundaries of political states, while some include multiple nations like the Anglican Church of the Southern Cone of America (Argentina, Bolivia, Chile, Paraguay, Peru, and Uruguay). Worldwide, each Anglican province is independent, yet interrelated like a global family of churches.

THE ANGLICAN COMMUNION

Together, each province makes up the worldwide Anglican Communion, which is a global family of autonomous national provinces in a reciprocal relationship with one another. Perhaps the greatest strength of the Anglican Communion is the way in which each province works together for the greater good of the communion, despite significant disagreements on certain issues. Diversity is a strength. In the end, Anglicanism offers a way of belonging. To be an Anglican is to belong to a large family of more than eighty million people from every continent spread across one hundred sixty-one countries. The Anglican tradition provides order, structure, and support to its members in order to ensure the proclamation of the gospel.

Historically the Archbishop of Canterbury is seen as the spiritual

ORDER: ANGLICAN HOLY ORDERS AND STRUCTURE

leader and the head of the Anglican Communion. He is first among equals of the other Primates of the various provinces of the Anglican Communion. In addition, he is the Primate of all England and Diocesan Bishop of the Diocese of Canterbury. Although he has a place of honor among other Primates, he has no authority over any other province other than his own. The current Archbishop of Canterbury, Justin Welby reminds us that "as Anglicans we are both catholic and reformed: committed to a shared life together (our catholicity) yet retaining local autonomy (having nether pope nor curia). Thus we are deeply affected by one another, even though our diverse provinces remain technically independent and autonomous."[8] Archbishop Welby has worked to bring reconciliation and healing to the fractures within the Anglican Communion. However, despite his best efforts the Anglican Communion remains deeply divided.

The reality is, the Anglican Communion has become increasingly divided over the last few decades. The best way to describe the current state of the Anglican Communion is like a family of churches that has experienced deep division that is similar to a painful divorce where the children have had to choose sides. The Anglican Communion's divisions and disagreements are very complex and painful. In 2003, the division became increasingly widened when The Episcopal Church consecrated a non-celibate homosexual as bishop. Since then, the Anglican Communion has wrestled with how to address questions of unity, authority, ecclesiology, and globalization. The response by many conservative Anglicans was the formation of the Global Anglican Future Conference (GAFCON) in 2008 and the Anglican Church in North America in 2009.[9]

The purpose of this section is not to try to explain all of the causes of these divisions (others have already done this), but to simply to acknowledge that they do exist.[10] In light of this fact, we need to remind ourselves that like a painful divorce, there are wounded people on all sides of the divide who love Jesus. Therefore, we need grace and humility as we look to the future of Anglicanism. As Anglicans, we are deeply connected to other believers from around the world, and what happens in one province affects another. Time will tell what the future will hold for the worldwide Anglican Communion, but I believe that the historic marks of orthodoxy can provide a means of unity, fellowship, and mission across the Anglican Communion.

CONCLUSION

In conclusion, in a world of disorder and chaos I believe that the structure of Anglicanism is a gift. To be an Anglican is to be submitted to an ordered way of life and belonging. Anglicanism provides a framework that undergirds our faith, not a straight-jacket that binds us. To be an Anglican means that you are a baptized member of a local church led by ordained priests who faithfully administer the sacraments of baptism and the Eucharist. To be an Anglican is to be connected to a local diocese under the spiritual leadership of a diocesan bishop. I often tell people that "to be Anglican is to have a bishop." In my opinion, this is one of the great blessings of the Anglican tradition, spiritual authority. To be an Anglican is to be connected to a national province of churches that are related to one another in a geographic region.

Finally, to be an Anglican is to be a part of a very large and at times, messy family of Christians scattered throughout the world called the Anglican Communion. Welcome to the family! Whatever the future of Anglicanism is, I believe it will be global.[11] Anglicanism truly is a global faith with members in every part of the world. Anglicans around the world and in different provinces are working together in common way, through a common faith, for a common mission to advance the gospel of Jesus Christ. More and more, Westerners have to take the posture of learners. In particular, there is so much to learn from the global Anglican Communion. Former Archbishop of Uganda Henry Luke Orombi recognized this shift when he proclaimed, "The younger churches of Anglican Christianity will shape what it means to be Anglican." [12] The global nature of the Anglican church reminds us that the church is like a mosaic that is made up of many colors. Each piece makes it a beautiful masterpiece. Today there are many different expressions and types of Anglican churches, and I believe that is a good thing for all of us.

DISCUSSION QUESTIONS

1. Anglicanism is an orderly tradition. What is the historic threefold order of ministry, and why is it still relevant today? Explain the roles of bishop, priest, and deacon.

2. What significance does the role of a bishop play in the life of the Anglican Communion?

3. What is the unique function and purpose of the local church in the overall life of Anglicanism?

4. What are a diocese and a province, and how do they relate to one another?

5. Why is it important that the voice of Anglican beliefs and practices be a global rather than a centralized voice?

CLOSING PRAYER

O God, you made us in your own image and redeemed us through Jesus your Son: Look with compassion on the whole human family; take away the arrogance and hatred which infect our hearts; break down the walls that separate us; unite us in bonds of love; and work through our struggle and confusion to accomplish your purposes on earth; that, in your good time, all nations and races may serve you in harmony around your heavenly throne; through Jesus Christ our Lord. Amen.[13]

RECOMMENDED READING

A Priest's Handbook: The Ceremonies of the Church by Dennis G. Michno

An Introduction to World Anglicanism by Bruce Kaye

Next Christendom: The Coming of Global Christianity by Philip Jenkins

The Study of Anglicanism edited by Stephen Sykes, John Booty, and Jonathan Knight

The New Faces of Christianity: Believing the Bible in the Global South by Philip Jenkins

The Christian Priest Today by Michael Ramsey

The Future of Orthodox Anglicanism edited by Gerald R. McDermott

The Gospel and the Catholic Church: Recapturing a Biblical Understanding of the Church as the Body of Christ by Michael Ramsey

CHAPTER 8
MISSION: THE ANGLICAN WAY OF MISSION

"Anglicanism is an inherently missionary Christian tradition."
—Archbishop Drexel Gomez

WE LIVE IN an increasingly post-Christian world where we can't assume that Christianity is the dominant force in our culture. Timothy C. Tennent, president of Asbury Theological Seminary, recently welcomed incoming seminary students by saying, "Welcome to life on the fastest growing mission field in the world: North America."[1] Churches in North America and Europe are now witnessing a growing number of people who are radically unchurched.[2] In the United States alone, there are around 180 million who have no connection to a local church, making it one of the fastest growing mission fields in the Western Hemisphere.[3] It is estimated that six hundred and sixty to seven hundred thousand people leave the traditional church every year.[4] These are sobering statistics, indicating that massive cultural shifts are on the horizon for today's church.

> *"When I began attending this church, I was brand new to my faith. I did not have a strong grasp on the differences between denominations, and frankly, I did not think it was that big of a deal. Some Christians baptized babies; some did not. Some baptized with a sprinkle while others dunked. I thought that pretty much covered it. With the support of this new community and*

leadership and an unquenchable desire to draw closer to God, I quickly learned more about Christian faith and practice, church history, the differences among denominations, and about Anglicanism, in particular."—SUNITA THEISS[5]

What, if anything, can we learn from an ancient tradition like Anglicanism for today's church that is facing an increasingly global, multicultural, and secularized world? I believe that the answer is a lot. It could be argued that the history of Anglicanism is the history of missions. The mission of the church drives the heart and soul of Anglicanism. Over the centuries, many great missionary thought leaders have come out of the Anglican tradition, such as John Wesley, William Wilberforce, Henry Venn, Roland Allen, and Lesslie Newbigin to name a few.

In this chapter, I want to show that there is something within the very DNA of the Anglican tradition—rooted in the sacraments—that prepares and compels believers to join in the mission of God. The sacraments and liturgy have a profoundly missional element to them, which drive the church toward mission rather than away from it. We will examine several missional movements within our Anglican history. In doing so, we will see that mission is at the very heart of our Anglican heritage.

A LEGACY OF MISSION

As we look at the story of Anglicanism, mission and church planting are at the very heart of our Anglican heritage. Bede's *Ecclesiastical History of the English People* records the early missionary expansion of the Church of England.[6] One of the earliest examples took place in AD 633, when King Oswald of Northumbria desired to bring

MISSION: THE ANGLICAN WAY OF MISSION

Christianity to his kingdom and requested the monks of Iona to come and minister to his people.[7] The first monk who was sent, Corman, met with little success. It was decided that St. Aidan would be sent out from Iona to establish Christianity in the North of England. Aidan arrived in the North of England around AD 635 accompanied by 12 other monks. King Oswald gave him the small island of Lindisfarne, (also known as Holy Island) as a home base to establish his monastic work. Lindisfarne provided both solitude and a base for missionary work, being cut off from the mainland except for twice a day during the periods of low tide. The missionary monks who trained on Lindisfarne went out from there and helped bring the gospel to much of Anglo-Saxon England, especially in the North of England.[8]

Anglicanism expanded through the work of mission organizations of the Church of England such as the Society for Promoting Christian Knowledge (SPCK, founded in 1698) and the Society for the Propagation of the Gospel in Foreign Parts (SPG, founded in 1701). The Church Missionary Society (CMS) was founded by a group of evangelical activists that included William Wilberforce in 1799. The founders of CMS were committed to the abolition of the slave trade, social reform, and world evangelization. Beginning with Sierra Leone in 1804, CMS sent missionaries to indigenous people around the world. During the mid-19th century, Henry Venn was the Secretary of the CMS whose missionary model for "indigenous church" was designed to help overseas churches become self-sustainable. These early mission societies sowed the seeds for what is now the worldwide Anglican Communion. Today, there are hundreds of Anglican mission organizations, such as Anglican Frontier Missions, that are helping to spread the gospel throughout the world.

Another unique historic example of Anglican mission was the Wesleyan revival, which was an Anglican renewal movement that started in the Church of England and quickly grew into a worldwide missionary movement. God raised up Anglican clergymen John Wesley, Charles Wesley, George Whitfield, and others to help usher in the Great Awakening and to begin a renewal movement that later came to be known as Methodism. Starting from only a handful of people, Methodism established hundreds of societies in England and the United States. Some historians have suggested that this revival helped save England from a bloody revolution like the one France would shortly experience.[9] By the time of John Wesley's death in 1791, the Methodists had become a global church movement with more than 70,000 members in England and more than 40,000 in the new United States and other mission stations around the world.[10] Even though it eventually separated from the Church of England, the Methodist movement still stands out as an Anglican renewal movement with many lessons that we can still learn today.

ANGLO-CATHOLIC MISSION

Even the Anglo-Catholic revival of the 19th century was missional. John Henry Newman served for a short period as the secretary of the Church Missionary Society. While serving in Oxford, he planted a church at Littlemore. Edward Pusey personally helped several church plants throughout England. A number of Anglo-Catholic priests led the way of doing mission work to improve the housing conditions for the residents in the slums. Anglo-Catholic priests responded by planting new churches that attempted to meet the pressing needs of their day in innovative new ways. Many of the church plants started in homes, bars, schools, and engaged their local communities in fresh new ways. Many of the church planters went into the highways and hedges to go where the church was not or had not been, such as the slums of the East End of London.[11]

Stories abound of the slum priests who ministered to the poorest of the poor. Anglo-Catholics ministered among the urban poor in the places that needed them most. Many of them used nontraditional methods to reach people in their local context. One of my favorites was Reverend Arthur Osborne Montgomery Jay (1858–1945), who had been selected by the bishop of London as Vicar of Holy Trinity, Shoreditch, in late 1886 to reach the outcasts of the Old Nichol district. When Jay entered the parish, there was no church building. Instead, services were held in the loft of a stable that smelled of manure. Jay's first service on New Year's Eve only had 14 people. However, within ten years, he had raised enough money to build a church, social club, lodging house, and gymnasium. By the late 1880s, Jay and others had come to realize that one of the best ways to engage poor men was through boxing. To combat his critics, Jay once preached a sermon at Holy Trinity called "May a Christian Box?" Some of the boxers who got their start in Jay's gym were Jack the Bender, Lord Dunfunkus, Old Squash, Tommy Irishman, Scrapper, and Donkey. Jay's story shows us that there is no place where the church cannot go to reach people for Christ.

EAST AFRICAN REVIVAL
One of the greatest influences upon the growth of Christianity in Africa came in the form of the East African Revival in the 1930s. This movement swept throughout the African nations of Uganda, Rwanda, Kenya, Tanzania, Burundi, and Congo, and transformed the lives of millions of people with the power of the gospel. One of

the leaders of this movement, Dr. Joe Church, was an Evangelical Anglican missionary doctor who spent decades working in Rwanda and Uganda.

The revival began within the Anglican Church of Uganda through a partnership between Joe Church and several Ugandan evangelists. It quickly spread to other churches of Kenya and of Tanzania during the 1940s and 1950s. Dr. Church played an important role in documenting the East African Revival through its early years. The revival focused upon the centrality of the saving power of Jesus Christ and the revival reaped an unimaginable reward.

Drexel Gomez, former archbishop of the West Indies, described the importance of the East African Revival in a speech called "On Being Anglican in the Twenty-First Century." He proclaimed the following:

> The East African Revival, little noticed in the 1920's and 1930's, had quietly planted the seeds of vital Christian faith within the Anglican Church throughout the Great Lakes region of the Rift valley, through mainly lay evangelism. And in the 1960's, after independence and the rise of indigenous church leadership, and in the 1970's and to this day, its fires spread rapidly. As with similar movements and attitudes in West Africa, these fires have so aroused the witness of the church as completely to overturn the dismal predictions of just 40 years ago. Rather than waning in the face of a modern surge in either secularism or Islam, Christianity in its Anglican tradition has instead awakened to the power of the gospel to change and be taken in by local Christians, within the order and structure of the church's life, quietly erected and nurtured

over decades...It is only against this historic backdrop of mission and revival that we can make sense of the changing shape of the Anglican Communion and, in particular, the recent coming of age of what is known as "the Global South" and the rise in global Christianity of, in the title of Philip Jenkins' influential work, "The Next Christendom."[12]

Without a doubt, the East African Revival represents a historic movement of Anglicanism that can still be felt today, especially in the Global South. More recent examples include the explosive growth of Christianity in Africa that has led to the planting of thousands of new churches across the continent. Prior to becoming the first dean and president of Trinity School for Ministry, Bishop Alfred Stanway served as a missionary bishop in Tanzania from 1951 to 1971. During that time, he helped oversee the planting of one thousand new churches. That's one new church every seven days!

NEWBIGIN AND TRINITARIAN MISSION

Anglicans can also claim one of the most significant missionary thinkers of the 20th century, James Edward Lesslie Newbigin (1909–98). Newbigin was a missionary, theologian, author, and pastor who was born in Newcastle-upon-Tyne, England. He spent nearly 40 years on the mission field, where he served as bishop of Madurai, India for over a decade. When Newbigin returned to Britain after forty years from India, he was shocked to find how much the Western world had changed. When he left, the church had a prominent place in the culture and was the dominant religious force in the West. However, when he returned to England he found that the West had become the new mission field. Rather than embracing cultural secularism,

Newbigin argued that the church needed to recover a robust Trinitarian theology of the mission of God.

For Newbigin, one of the primary issues at stake was the authority of the church's mission. He resisted the temptation to ground authority in the dominant secular culture as many Christians had done. This rendered the church ineffective and anemic. He determined, "Every proposal to seek authority elsewhere than in the gospel itself must lead us astray. The only proper response to the question 'By what authority?' is the announcement of the gospel itself."[13] Mission does not begin with us, but with the triune God. While many base their understanding of mission on old Christendom models, Christians needed to rediscover that the mission of the church can only be rightly understood, "if we see it as the work of God who has sent His Son and given His Spirit, as a sharing through the spirit in the obedience of the Son to the Father, as a participation in the spirit who enables us to know God as Father and to confess Christ as Lord, and to wait with assurance and patience for the coming of His Kingdom."[14]

He taught that Jesus Christ, the Son of God is the embodiment of mission in the World. In many ways, Jesus Christ was the first missionary being sent from the Father. According to Lesslie Newbigin, "The mission of Jesus was not only to proclaim the Kingdom of God, but also to embody the presence of the Kingdom of God in his own person."[15] The kingdom of God was made known in Jesus' proclamation of the gospel: "'The time has come,' he said. 'The kingdom of God has come near. Repent and believe the good news!'" (Mark 1:15). Through the incarnation of Jesus, the gospel is not only proclaimed, but embodied in the person of Jesus Christ, the Son of God. In His own words, Jesus proclaims, "As You sent Me into the world, I also have sent them into the world" (John 17:18). Being that

Christ is the head of the church and the church is the body of Christ, mission is our response to the sending commission of Jesus.

Newbigin also argued, "Mission is not just something that the church does; it is something that is done by the Spirit, who is himself the witness, who changes both the world and the church, who always goes before the church in its missionary journey."[16] For him, "Mission is not self-propagation," but it is rather the work of the "free, sovereign, living power of the Spirit of God."[17] Newbigin reminds us that the third person in the Trinity, the doctrine of the Holy Spirit, offers an important contribution for the contemporary mission of the church today. The Spirit always points to Jesus Christ and Jesus always points to the Father. A robust Trinitarian approach to missiology offers us a holistic understanding of mission that is rooted in the Father, Son, and Spirit who work together and invite us to join them on their triune mission in the world.

NEW FIRE IN LONDON

Today as we look around the Anglican world, we see that mission is not a thing of the past. There are many wonderful contemporary examples of how Anglicans are doing mission throughout England, North America, and around the world. In the midst of rapid decline in church attendance nationally, there is a missional movement brewing in the Church of England that is bringing renewal to churches and communities across England. In 2015, the former Bishop of London Richard Chartres delivered a lecture entitled "New Fire in London" in which he talked about the growth within the Diocese of London through church planting. He shared the following commitment to mission: "We are pledged to establish 100 new worshiping communities in the Diocese in the next five years."[18] To help accomplish this vision, Ric Thorpe was consecrated as Bishop of Islington with a special focus on church planting in London. Thorpe now leads the Gregory Centre for Church Multiplication to support leaders and church teams across London, England and beyond as they look to multiply disciples, churches and networks.[19] His passion is to make disciple-making leaders in new and revitalized churches in London and across England. "My main work is culture change," he says. "I'm trying to help people imagine themselves more as a missionary church, as opposed to just sustaining what has always gone before."[20] Thorpe's goal is to see disciples, leaders, and churches that multiply everywhere.

Another significant trend in Anglican mission that developed in London is the Alpha Course, which is an evangelistic course that seeks to introduce the basics of Christianity in the setting of a meal and discussion group. According to the Alpha website, "Alpha is a series of interactive sessions that freely explore the basics of the Christian faith. No pressure. No follow up. No charge."[21] Alpha courses are taking place in churches, homes, coffee houses, and a wide variety of other locations. Alpha was started in 1977 at Holy Trinity Brompton in London. In 1990, Nicky Gumbel, a curate at Holy Trinity, took over running the course, which has since become an international phenomenon.

Since its inception, over 24 million people have used Alpha in over 100 countries. Currently, Alpha is taught around the world by all major Christian denominations including Roman Catholic, Anglican, Baptist, Methodist, Lutheran, Orthodox, and Pentecostal. Many people have endorsed Alpha, like television adventurer Bear Grylls, who said, "Alpha was the best thing I ever did. It helped me answer some huge questions and find a simple empowering faith in my life."²² Alpha continues to be an effective tool that God is using to reach people for Christ around the world.

FRESH EXPRESSIONS

The Fresh Expressions (FX) movement represents another example of Anglican mission that has resulted in hundreds of new congregations being formed alongside more traditional churches. A fresh expression is "a form of church for our changing culture, established primarily for the benefit of people who are not yet members of any church."²³ Since it began in England in the early 2000s, the Fresh Expressions movement has resulted in the birth of more than three-thousand new communities alongside existing churches in the UK.²⁴

In 2003, the former Archbishop of Canterbury Rowan Williams called for a "mixed economy" of church that would include both traditional and fresh expressions of church to meet the new challenges of a post-Christian and post-modern context. In his own words, "We have begun to recognize that there are many ways in which the reality of 'church' can exist… These may be found particularly in the development of a mixed economy of Church life."²⁵ The phrase "fresh expressions" comes from the preface to the Declaration of Assent, which Church of England ministers make at their ordination to affirm the "faith the Church is called upon to proclaim afresh in each generation."²⁶ "Fresh expressions" echoes these words and suggests "something new or enlivened is happening, but also suggests connection to history and the developing story of God's work in the Church."²⁷

So, are fresh expressions actually making a difference? According to the Church of England's most recent research, they are. The Church Army's Research Unit for the Church Commissioners carried out a detailed study, in which Dr. George Lings, the Unit's Director, noted, "Nothing else, as a whole, in the Church of England has this level of missional impact and the adding of further ecclesial communities."[28] According to the Church of England's research of the last two decades, they found the following: a significant number of those who are a part of fresh expressions have no previous church background and, for every person sent to establish a fresh expression, at least another two- and- a- half are now present. That's a 250% increase over time.[29]

MISSION IN NORTH AMERICA

The United States has its own rich legacy of Anglican mission. Bishop Jackson Kemper (1789–1870) was the first missionary bishop who came to be known as the "bishop of the Whole Northwest."[30] As a missionary bishop, Kemper focused on working with Native American people, founding parishes and schools on the Western frontier. Another great example was priest, educator, and missionary Rev. James Lloyd Breck (1818–1876), who became known as the "apostle to the West." Under the direction of Bishop Jackson Kemper, he and two other classmates went to the frontier of Wisconsin to found Nashotah House, a seminary in the Anglo-Catholic tradition, in 1842. Throughout his lifetime, Breck worked tirelessly, teaching, training, and helping to found missions and schools including Seabury Seminary in other parts of the Western region. Breck is known as "The Apostle of the Wilderness."[31]

Today, a fresh mission movement is happening in cities and communities all across the United States. Several significant missional expressions have emerged through the Anglican Church in North America in recent years to fulfill its mission to "reach North America with the transforming love of Jesus Christ," and it has initiated a movement to plant Anglican churches across North America. In his opening provincial address, Archbishop Bob Duncan issued a call to plant one thousand new churches. Since that time, hundreds of church planters are beginning to step forward to answer the call. While many denominations are maintaining the status quo, the Anglican Church in North America is committed to starting new churches. Since its inception in 2009, the Anglican Church in North America has planted hundreds of new churches across the United States in a variety of different contexts. At the heart of this is Always Forward, which is a collaborative effort of the ACNA to promote planting new Gospel-centered, sacramental, missional churches throughout North America.

One of the most significant missional thinkers in North America is Bishop Todd Hunter. Hunter leads Churches for the Sake of Others (C4SO), a diocese committed to planting new Anglican churches. He hasn't always been an Anglican, having been involved with planting churches for decades, serving as past President of Alpha USA, and being the former National Director for the Association of Vineyard Churches. He has written several significant books, including *Christianity Beyond Belief: Following Jesus for the Sake of Others*, *Giving Church Another Chance*, *The Outsider Interviews*, *The Accidental Anglican*, *Our Favorite Sins*, and *Our Character at Work*.

In many ways, his previous experience has prepared him to be the missionary bishop that he is today. Bishop Hunter also leads the Telos Collective, which seeks to gather Anglican leaders from every diocese who think like missionaries and are committed to reach 21st century North America for Christ. At the heart of his mission and the Telos Collective is to equip missional leaders to work at the intersection of gospel and culture. Hunter describes the missional thrust of Anglicanism in the following way:

> The Book of Common Prayer is going missional! Leading us by prayer into a kingdom and missional worldview, I see the Book of Common Prayer shaping the community of Jesus one life at a time, as we become his cooperative friends, living in creative goodness, through the power of the Holy Spirit, for the sake of others.[32]

MULTIETHNIC MISSION

One stereotype about Anglicanism in North America is that it is, well, too "Anglo." All that is changing. One of the most exciting and important works that is happening in North America is the Anglican Multi-Ethnic Network (AMEN), which is "dedicated to encouraging the church to better embody the universal saving power of the gospel through planting multi-ethnic churches or increasing the presence of people of color in existing churches."[33] AMEN is helping Anglican churches address the ongoing concerns of people of color, especially issues of social justice. As North America increasingly becomes more and more multicultural, the work of the Anglican Multi-Ethnic Network is going to be essential for the future of helping Anglican churches in North America become more diverse and represent the context.

Rev. Dr. Esau McCaulley is professor of New Testament at Wheaton College and an Anglican priest in the ACNA. He is also a leading voice in the African American community and often speaks on issues of diversity and culture. He believes that a growing number of African Americans are being drawn toward Anglicanism.

There has never been more interest from African Americans and other ethnic groups in joining the ACNA than there is now. Many have been burned by the culture wars in wider Evangelicalism and want something with a bit more generosity, but that maintains the theological clarity. Also, black people can fall in love with the liturgy just like anyone else. The Anglican tradition has a lot to offer all people. The question is whether we will be a hospitable home for them…If the ACNA cares about multiethnicity, it must also take seriously the African American Christian tradition and its historical combination of orthodoxy *and* orthopraxy.[34]

The Anglican church in the United States must become increasingly diverse if it is going to represent the nation. According to the Census, the USA will become "minority white" by 2045.[35] That means the future of the church in North America will be increasingly multiethnic and diverse. With more than 337 languages represented, the United States has become the most multicultural and multilingual nation on earth.[36] The challenge of reaching the numerous people groups is a result of the growing diaspora from other nations who have come to North America. These men and women are often difficult to reach due to various language, cultural, and ethnic boundaries. As we witness the globalization of North America, the nations on continents such as Africa, Asia, and South America are beginning to send missionaries to re-evangelize the West through church planting! British author Martin Robinson talks about some of these church planters from developing countries who are now coming to the West.[37] They have come from nations like Brazil, Haiti, Mexico, Nigeria, Dominican Republic, and Ethiopia, just to name a few.

As the West continues to experience globalization, a growing number of churches are beginning to focus on reaching people from various nationalities and ethnic backgrounds. For instance, in many urban contexts, churches will have to cross racial, cultural, and socioeconomic lines to reach their communities. Multiethnic ministry points to the beautiful picture promised in Revelation, where people from every nation, tribe, and language praise God in unison with one another. This portrait is essential to the Christian faith, and no matter what kind of church we attend or are thinking about planting, we should all find ways to reach across ethnic, racial, cultural, and economic barriers. Multiethnic Anglican churches will increasingly be the future of church in North America and around the world.

CONCLUSION

In conclusion, to be an Anglican is to be a part of a missionary movement that has a long and rich heritage of holistic mission. This rich heritage reminds us that God's love inspires us to be missionaries to the world around us. Many Anglicans around the world have adopted the Five Marks of Mission, which "express the Anglican Communion's common commitment to, and understanding of, God's holistic and integral mission."[38] I believe that these five marks offer the church a holistic model of mission for the 21st century. The Five Marks of Mission are:

1. To proclaim the Good News of the Kingdom

2. To teach, baptize and nurture new believers

3. To respond to human need by loving service

4. To transform unjust structures of society, to challenge violence of every kind and pursue peace and reconciliation

5. To strive to safeguard the integrity of creation, and sustain and renew the life of the earth

Every Christian, regardless of our tradition or background, can be missional by joining in God's mission through the Five Marks of Mission. Whether it be proclaiming the gospel in word and deed, making disciples, serving the needs of others, pursuing peace and reconciliation, or taking care of the creation, we can all share in the responsibility of fulfilling God's mission on the earth.

In conclusion, God's love inspires us all to be missionaries to the world around us. Theologian Emil Brunner said, "The church exists by mission just as fire exists by burning."[39] Mission begins at home, serving in our local church, and reaching our community. Every one of us can play a part in God's mission as we have been sent as missionaries to share the gospel in our present culture and to fulfill the Great Commission. Anglicanism has a missionary heritage that reminds us that the church is not an end in itself; the church is sent into the world to fulfill the mission of God. Whoever you are, wherever you are, we are all called to be missionaries of peace and to proclaim the gospel of Jesus Christ fresh to this generation! Mission is one of the greatest legacies of the Anglican tradition.

DISCUSSION QUESTIONS

1. How has Anglicanism been a missional tradition throughout the centuries?

2. What are some of the ways that Anglicanism is growing and thriving on mission around the world?

3. Are there unique ways in which the Anglican tradition engages in mission that are different from other traditions? If so, then explain why and how.

4. What, if anything, is important about the focus on multiethnic ministry today?

CLOSING PRAYERS

O God, our heavenly Father, you manifested your love by sending your only-begotten Son into the world, that all might live through him: Pour out your Spirit on your Church, that we may fulfill his command to preach the Gospel to all people. Send forth laborers into your harvest; defend them in all dangers and temptations; and hasten the time when the fullness of the Gentiles shall be gathered in, and faithful Israel shall be saved; through your Son Jesus Christ our Lord. Amen.[40]

RECOMMENDED READING

A History of Christian Missions by Stephen Neill

Evangelism and the Sovereignty of God by J. I. Packer

Evangelism in the Early Church by Michael Green

Marks of a Movement by Winfield Bevins

Missionary Methods: St. Paul's or Ours? by Roland Allen

The Celtic Way of Evangelism by George G. Hunter III

The Gospel in a Pluralist Society by Lesslie Newbigin

CHAPTER 9
CHARITY: EMBRACING THE ANGLICAN *VIA MEDIA*

"The truth is not in the middle, and not in one extreme;
but in both extremes."—CHARLES SIMEON

AS WE CLOSE OUT the book I want to end with the question, "How do we live into the tensions and paradoxes of the faith?" Most of us like everything neat and clean; however life and faith attract messiness. Becoming an Anglican has helped me embrace the tensions and paradoxes of the Christian faith that often lead to much chaos. A paradox is a seemingly self-contradictory declaration which is in fact true, and such paradoxes saturate the Scriptures: strength in weakness (see 2 Corinthians 12:10), receiving through giving (see Acts 20:35), freedom through serving (see Romans 6:18), gaining through losing (see Philippians 3:7–8), or living through dying (see John 12:24), to name a few.

Anglicanism is known for the *via media*, which is a Latin term that means "the middle way." The middle way allows us to synthesize great Christian truths into a central core, rather than focusing on extremes. In *Treatise on the Laws of Ecclesiastical Polity*, Richard Hooker (1544–1600) argued that Anglicanism retains the best of Roman Catholicism (liturgy and tradition) and Protestantism (authority of Scripture and justification). While a comprehensive, synthetic approach to the Christian faith has existed for centuries within the Anglican tradition, the concept of the *via media* became prominent among Anglicans in the nineteenth century with the writings of John Henry Newman.[1]

One of the best examples of a *via media* approach can be found in the life and ministry of John Wesley, who lived and died an Anglican priest. John Wesley's unique Evangelical Anglicanism comes to light in his ability to find a synthesis between radical extremes and paradoxes, such as divine sovereignty and free will, evangelical and sacramental, and saving and sanctifying grace.[2] To be an Anglican is to understand and to live in the tension of the paradoxes of the Christian faith by employing the *via media*.

The *via media* stands as one of Anglicanism's greatest gifts to the world. However, it seems that Anglicanism is in danger of losing its *via media*. Too often, contemporary Anglicanism feels politicized and polarizing, leaving little room for those of us in the middle, but as we look to both the past and the future, I believe that Anglicans desperately need to recover the *via media* for the sake of our church. Concurrently, theologian Alister McGrath argues that Anglicanism at its best avoids both fundamentalism and liberalism, the first of which rejects culture and the latter of which adopts too much culture.[3] In *The Renewal of Anglicanism*, he writes

> There is a real need for the reconstruction of a *via media*, which avoids the increasingly outmoded dialectic between 'catholic' and 'protestant', and addresses the *real* issue of today; the failure of both liberalism and fundamentalism to provide a relevant and responsible form of Christianity for today's world. One collapses into the world, the other refuses to have anything to do with it. If ever a *via media* was needed, it is now.[4]

I agree with McGrath that Anglicans need to recover the *via media*. Let me state for the record that I am neither a fundamentalist, nor a liberal, but I am an ordinary middle-of-the-road, orthodox Anglican. I don't think I am alone, and I would like to offer a few thoughts that might help us recover a vision for gracious orthodox Anglicanism in North America that holds to the *via media* that has a robust theology and is generous toward others with whom we disagree.

Perhaps the most practical way in which the Anglican tradition lives in tension comes as it seeks to bring together a variety of dimensions of the Christian faith.

At first, these may seem like opposing extremes, but in many ways these different streams are symbiotic and belong together. Anglicanism offers a balanced faith that brings together the best of the Christian traditions. This chapter will explore the unique balance of unity and diversity in Anglicanism through the *via media* and the importance of bringing together the different streams within Anglicanism, which include: Catholic, Evangelical, Broad, and Charismatic. At our best, these streams are not separate channels, but they come together in one river.

A CATHOLIC FAITH

Anglicans see themselves as a part of the "one, holy, catholic, and apostolic church." For many, the word "Catholic" evokes initial thoughts of the Roman Catholic Church. However, the word does not specifically refer to the modern Catholic Church of Rome. The word "catholic" (not capitalized) simply means "universal" and refers to the universal nature of the church. This notion of catholic has its origins in the writings of Paul, "There is one body, one Spirit . . .

one Lord, one faith, one baptism, one God and Father of all" (Eph. 4:4–6). There is only one true church, and it is made up of all true believers in Jesus Christ. For the remainder of the book I will use the word "catholic" to refer to the universal nature of the church.

In the middle of the twentieth century, Archbishop Geoffrey Fisher affirmed the Anglican position when he stated, "We have no doctrine of our own—we only possess the Catholic doctrine of the Catholic Church enshrined in the Catholic creeds, and those creeds we hold without addition or diminution."[5] As we have already seen, the Catholic dimension within Anglicanism was recovered by the Oxford Movement of the 19th century. By ascribing to these universal truths and traditions, Anglicanism recovers the beliefs and practices of the historic Christian faith, such as a strong emphasis on the Sacraments and the role of ordained ministry.

A modern Anglican who represents the catholic dimension of the Christian faith is Michael Ramsey. Ramsey was Archbishop of Canterbury from 1961–1974 and was also a significant theologian and champion for Christian unity. Raised as a congregationalist, Ramsay eventually became a high-church Anglican. He studied at Magdalene College, Cambridge, and was president of the Cambridge Union. He attended Cuddesdon Theological College and was ordained in 1928. He held a number of prominent positions, including professor of divinity at the Universities of Durham and Cambridge, Bishop of Durham, and Archbishop of York.

Ramsey was a well-loved Archbishop of Canterbury who worked hard to build ecumenical relationships with other Christian communions. While serving as Archbishop of Canterbury he served as president of the World Council of Churches from 1961 to 1968. In 1966, he had a historic meeting with Pope Paul VI, which was the first encounter between the leaders of the Roman Catholic and Anglican churches since their separation in 1534. This meeting was a significant development toward bringing the two historic churches back into dialogue.

Ramsey had a passion to call the church to embrace both the Catholic and Evangelical dimensions of the Christian faith. He believed that to separate the Catholic from the Evangelical was a false dichotomy that needed to be reconciled in the church. In *The Gospel and the Catholic Church*, Ramsey said:

> The Evangelical and the Catholic are utterly one. To understand the Catholic Church and its life and order is to see it as the utterance of the gospel of God; to understand the gospel of God is to share with all the saints in the building up of the one body of Christ. Hence these two aspects of Anglicanism cannot really be separated. It possesses a full Catholicity, only if it is faithful to the gospel of God; and it is fully Evangelical insofar as it upholds the church order wherein an important aspect of the gospel is set forth. . . . For the Anglican Church is committed not to a vague position wherein the Evangelical and the Catholic views are alternatives, but to the scriptural faith wherein both elements are of one.[6]

The catholic dimension of Anglicanism also reminds us that we belong to the larger body of Christ and that we should embrace the richness and great diversity in the various church traditions. As Christians, we can claim the riches of the various streams of Christendom from both the past and present. The various branches of the church around the world are like a mosaic or tapestry that consists of many colors and dimensions. Each fragment displays a different color, but in unison, these individual pieces portray a beautiful masterpiece. Likewise, today there are many different expressions and types of churches that are all a part of the Body of Christ. With theologian J. I. Packer, Anglicans would agree that we should "practice fellowship across the traditions, for the Holy Spirit has been with all God's people in all traditions in all centuries."[7]

AN EVANGELICAL FAITH

Anglicanism is not only Catholic; it is also Evangelical. People who consider themselves Evangelicals often toss this word around without any definitive characteristics. Because of its broad usage, we must ask, what exactly does it mean to be an Evangelical Anglican? The word *evangelical* comes from the Greek word *evangelion*, which our Bibles translate as "gospel" or "good news." At the most basic level, an Evangelical Anglican is one who believes in, has been converted by, and who shares the good news of Jesus Christ. In a sense, Anglicanism has always been evangelical. Evangelicalism reminds us of the centrality of the Bible, Jesus' death on a cross, and the importance of conversion, as well as evangelism. Such a heritage reminds us that we are all called to share the good news of Jesus' love and forgiveness with the world. You can find these hallmarks of Evangelicalism throughout Anglican history. From John and Charles Wesley to J. C. Ryle, the evangelical impulse has been alive in the Anglican tradition from the beginning until now. Contemporary Evangelical Anglicans include John Stott, N. T. Wright, Alister McGrath, Richard Turnbull, and J. I. Packer.

"Anglicanism has stewarded many practices from the early Christians, cultivating them and re-setting them in beautiful ways. One might even say that the Anglican gift to the wider

Body of Christ is their prayer book. As I've visited and participated in other historic Christian worship practices, I've gleaned something from each, but have found something special within Anglicanism." —GLENN PACKIAM[8]

Evangelicalism elevates the essentials of the Christian faith, because without them we cease to be Christian. This is what has happened to many of the declining churches of the West. Paul Zahl, former dean of the Cathedral Church of the Advent, wrote, "For the renewal of Anglicanism to take place, it is required that a renewal of Christianity within Anglicanism take place."[9] You can't be a Christian without Jesus Christ! As Christians, we need the Scriptures, we need Jesus Christ as our Savior, we need the Holy Spirit, we need a conversion experience, we need fellowship, and we need to share our faith with others.

The unique blend of Catholic and Evangelical roots stands as one of the great reasons many evangelicals are drawn to Anglicanism. Elizabeth Peterson and her husband, Joel, both came from evangelical non-denominational backgrounds. However, it was not until they returned from the mission field to attend Asbury Seminary in Wilmore, Kentucky, that they became Anglicans. In Anglicanism, they encountered Christ in the Word and the sacraments. The unique synergy of the Catholic and Evangelical dimensions is one of the things that influenced their decision to make Anglicanism their spiritual home. Elizabeth describes their experience in the following way:

On a hot, August Sunday afternoon in 2012, at 4:00 pm, we walked into the service of St. Patrick's Anglican Church in Lexington, Kentucky. Thankfully, we received a very clear worship guide so we could join in the liturgy easily. We followed along and read the notes explaining why we were doing what we were doing. I managed to sit, stand, and kneel without being out of step, although it took months for me to manage to cross myself at the right time. The priest did the one thing that mattered to me more than anything else: he preached the gospel of Jesus Christ clearly, compellingly, and in a way that both grew my love for Jesus and assured me deeply of His love for me. Since then, we've been making our home in the Anglican Communion. It's a home that welcomes me as an evangelical follower of Jesus. Yes, the sermon preached may not be the center of the service for Anglicans but it is central to how I grow as a disciple. Yet we've also found a home that has changed us—the thought of coming to the Table and receiving communion only once a month or even once a year (about as often as one team we were a part of partook of the Lord's Supper) is no longer tenable for me.[10]

Once we see Anglicanism as something like a family, then we can ask what holds this family together and what accounts for its diversity. Anglicanism stands within the evangelical tradition because we have absolute tenets of the faith, but it also holds firmly to Catholic foundations in order to have enough room to allow others to interpret the Scriptures for themselves, provided they remain within the evangelical core. With God as our center, through unity and diversity, the Anglican community has a unique dynamism.

A BROAD FAITH

A third movement within Anglicanism that emerged in the

mid-nineteenth century that sought to embody the comprehensiveness of Anglican tradition is often referred to as the "Broad Church Movement." Broad Church is a term that appeared in the mid-nineteenth century to describe an approach to the doctrine and worship of the Church of England that was more tolerant and liberal than the views of the existing Anglo-Catholics (or High Churchmen) on one hand and the Evangelicals (or Low Churchmen) on the other hand. The term is thought to have originated with poet and educationist A. H. Clough. A number of leaders are associated with the early years of the Broad Church movement, including, F. D. Maurice, Thomas Arnold, S. T. Coleridge, Benjamin Jowett, and A. P. Stanley.

Hallmarks of the Broad Church movement include a desire to engage in the general welfare of the life of the English nation through social justice. The Broad Church Movement helped focus the church's energy on social reforms which included feeding the poor and education. The Broad Church movement also had a desire for the Church of England to be more comprehensive rather than exclusive. Those who identified with the Broad Church movement in its early years sought for the church to embrace some of the social and intellectual changes of the new modern world. Many of these changes were brought on by the advent of German biblical criticism and Darwin's theory of evolution. This included a growing openness to intellectual freedom that tended toward progressive and liberal theological perspectives. Over time, the Broad Church movement came to be associated with the liberal side of Anglicanism, which can especially be found in parts of the Episcopal Church and the Church of England today. However, the Broad Church stream is nether conservative or liberal, rather it is marked by a desire to be comprehensive rather than exclusive.

A CHARISMATIC FAITH

Another important stream within Anglicanism is commonly known as the Charismatic stream, which reminds us of the importance of the person and work of the Holy Spirit. The Spirit played an important role in the life and ministry of the early church, and one cannot possibly understand the explosive growth of the New Testament church without first understanding the important role of the Holy Spirit. The Spirit plays the initiatory role in personal salvation, spiritual formation, and the general spread of the gospel. Without Him, it is impossible for individuals or the church to grow in Christ. The doctrine of the Holy Spirit has a distinct contribution to make to the contemporary church.

As we scan the pages of church history, we see the Holy Spirit's presence within the church in all eras. In more recent times, Anglicanism has been touched by the charismatic movement into North America and the British Isles. In 1960, Episcopal priest Dennis Bennett announced from the pulpit of St. Mark's Episcopal Church in Van Nuys, California, that he had been filled with the Holy Spirit. This set off a spark that ignited the charismatic renewal in mainline churches across North America. Around the same time, Michel Harper, who was a curate at All Souls, Langham Place, in London's West End, had a similar experience and became one of the primary leaders of the charismatic movement in the Church of England. Today, one of the largest charismatic churches in England is Holy Trinity Brompton, located in the heart of London. Holy Trinity Brompton is best known for the Alpha Course, which has been used in dozens of countries and hundreds of denominations, and has helped introduce millions of people to Christ.[11]

One example of a new church that is embracing the Charismatic stream is Trinity Anglican Mission in Atlanta, Georgia. Trinity is reaching hundreds of young adults in their twenties and thirties by engaging in ancient forms of liturgical worship and prayer. Trinity started a few years ago as a charismatic Vineyard church. Their spiritual journey eventually led them to become an Anglican church that embraces charismatic, evangelical, and sacramental dimensions of the Christian faith. They describe themselves as being "liturgical" and valuing the longevity of historic tradition, the rhythms of the church calendar, the consistency of a lectionary-based teaching plan, and having a connection to the global church. Trinity considers itself a three-streams church. According to their rector Kris McDaniel,

> When we say that we are "evangelical" we mean that we take seriously God's command to speak about and live like Jesus. We preach and teach from the Bible because we believe it is the inspired word of God, and our desire is for all people to enter into a saving relationship with Jesus. . . . When we say that we are "liturgical" we mean that we value the longevity of historic tradition, the rhythms of the church calendar, the consistency of a lectionary-based teaching plan, and our connection to the global church. . . . When we say that we are "charismatic" we mean that we believe God is present and active among His people. We anticipate the work of the Holy Spirit in the life of the church for the conviction of sin, the illumination of truth, and the restoration of all things.[12]

CLARITY AND CHARITY

The various streams are especially relevant today because the Catholic, Evangelical, Broad, and Charismatic dimensions of the faith belong together and are a gift to the body of Christ. By themselves, they can diverge into their own form of sectarianism. The Catholic dimension by itself can lead to ritualism. The Evangelical dimension by itself can lead to fundamentalism. The Broad Church dimension by itself can lead to liberalism. The Charismatic dimension by itself can lead to Charismania.

In Anglicanism, one finds a place to live out these diverse dimensions of the faith together in a beautiful tapestry. When these dimensions are woven together, they offer us a balanced model for the Christian life and practice. Walking this balance isn't always easy. In the words of Rev. Dr. Les Fairfield, "Each one extrapolates the gospel in a specific direction. No strand is dispensable. Other Christian bodies have often taken one strand to an extreme. By God's grace, the Anglican tradition has held the streams in creative tension. This miracle of unity is a treasure worth keeping."[13]

The Catholic, Evangelical, Broad, and Charismatic divide is just the beginning of the diversity within Anglicanism. There are, of course, many other issues and ways in which the church is deeply divided. Whether it is between conservatives and liberals, over women's ordination, or the meaning and nature of the sacraments, Christians can and do disagree. Diversity is nothing new to Anglicanism. Anglicans have always prided themselves in being a tradition that is roomy and that embraces diversity, sometimes to a fault. Author Richard H. Schmidt warned that "tolerance and inclusiveness can easily become a mere 'anything goes' laxity, a moral and intellectual flabbiness."[14] However, the openness to diversity within Anglicanism is also one of its greatest gifts.

I believe that clarity and charity is the orthodox Anglican way. In a world full of denominational divisiveness, Anglican comprehensiveness can be a model. The late evangelical Anglican John Stott argued for comprehensiveness without compromise. He proclaimed, "The way of separation is to pursue truth at the expense of unity. The way of compromise is to pursue unity at the expense of truth. The way of comprehension is to pursue truth and unity simultaneously, that is, to pursue the kind of unity recommended by Christ and his apostles, namely unity in truth."[15] What we need is a gracious comprehensiveness that is orthodox and committed to the essentials of the historic Christian faith, yet focused on loving those who disagree with us. I like the way that Fleming Rutledge describes being orthodoxy, yet generous. She says,

> We cannot do without orthodoxy, for everything else must be tested against it, but that orthodox (traditional, classical) Christian faith should by definition always be generous as our God is generous; lavish in his creation, binding himself in an unconditional covenant, revealing himself in the calling of a people, self-sacrificing in the death of his Son, prodigal in the gifts of the Spirit, justifying the ungodly and indeed, offending the "righteous" by the indiscriminate nature of his favor. True Christian orthodoxy therefore cannot be narrow, pinched, or defensive but always spacious, adventurous and unafraid.[16]

In short, we need to speak the truth in love. Or, as I said in the introduction, we need both clarity and charity. Many times, our arguments and disagreements can come across as unloving toward others and, in the end, can hinder our witness to the world. We need to learn to talk with those with whom we disagree. Jesus reminds us in John 13:35, "By this all people will know that you are my disciples, if you have love for one another." We will be known by our love. If we must disagree, then let us do so in a loving, Christ-like way. Sometimes we must be willing to lay aside our personal and institutional biases for the sake of Christian unity and mission, learning how to live and work together to reach a radically unchurched world with the gospel message of Jesus Christ.

The different streams of Anglicanism remind us that not everyone looks, acts, or thinks alike. Anglican churches come in all shapes and sizes and are very diverse; ranging from Anglo-Catholics who are more high church, employing a more ceremonial and expanded liturgy, to Evangelical Anglicans who are typically more low church, employing fewer ceremonial practices. Regardless of worship styles, Anglicans are united in the essential "catholic" doctrines of the Christian faith. This understanding is why Bishop Phillip Brooks once described Anglicanism as "the roomiest church in Christendom."[17] Although we don't always see alike, we can agree on the essentials of the faith and join together for the common cause of Christ. More than ever before, we need to learn to work together for the sake of the gospel.

DISCUSSION QUESTIONS

1. How would you describe the Anglican *via media*?

2. How does the Anglican tradition balance what is found in the different streams (Evangelical, Charismatic, Broad, and Catholic)?

3. What are some historic and modern examples of the three streams at work within the life of the Anglican tradition?

4. How can the different streams be a means to unite the various expressions of the church?

CLOSING PRAYER

O God the Father of our Lord Jesus Christ, our only Savior, the Prince of Peace: Give us grace seriously to lay to heart the great dangers we are in by our unhappy divisions; take away all hatred and prejudice, and whatever else may hinder us from godly union and concord; that, as there is but one Body and one Spirit, one hope of our calling, one Lord, one Faith, one Baptism, one God and Father of us all, so we may be all of one heart and of one soul, united in one holy bond of truth and peace, of faith and charity, and may with one mind and one mouth glorify thee; through Jesus Christ our Lord. Amen.[18]

RECOMMENDED READING

Anglicanism by Stephen Neill

Anglicanism: A Very Short Introduction by Mark Chapman

Evangelicals on the Canterbury Trail: Why Evangelicals Are Attracted to the Liturgical Church by Robert Webber

Gospel and the Catholic Church by Michael Ramsey

Of the Laws of Ecclesiastical Polity by Richard Hooker

The Apology of the Church of England by John Jewel

The Living Church by John Stott

CONCLUSION

> "Anglicanism is a living tradition, rather than a petrified fossil which bears only the marks of the past and has lost any ability to grow and develop in response to present conditions."
> —Allister McGrath

AS WE COME TO THE END of this journey, I hope you've been inspired by the breadth and depth of the Anglican tradition. These are but a few reasons why so many people from around the world have come to embrace the Anglican way. As J. I. Packer has said, "Anglicanism embodies the richest, truest, wisest heritage in all Christendom."[1] The Anglican tradition has enriched the faith of millions of Christians around the world for hundreds of years and still has the power to offer a vibrant, healthy, life-giving faith for our generation and generations to come.

Before we end, I want to make clear that I am not saying we should simply perpetuate the traditions of the past. Many denominations and churches are living in the past, thinking that if they could just return to the good old days everything would be all right. Trying to perpetuate the successes of the past is the reason many of our churches are empty and void of youth. On the contrary, the Anglican way shows us how the past, present, and future can come together through common prayer and worship. In Anglicanism, the church of the past can speak to the present, while the church of the present can reach into the future with a faith that is rooted and grounded in Christ in a dynamic way.

Throughout this book, I have offered an introduction to the history, faith, worship, and structure of the Anglican tradition. However, more than that, I have tried to offer a gracious invitation for newcomers to come and see how an ancient faith can be relevant for today's world. As I mentioned in the introduction, a growing number of Christians from various backgrounds are beginning to open up the treasure chest of church history to find ancient tools and practices to help them live out the faith in a postmodern world. That is not to say that Anglicanism is the only way Christians should live out their faith; neither is it for everyone.

I have also tried to paint a vision for the future of Anglicanism that is neither fundamentalist nor progressive—one that is historically rooted and modern; orthodox and gracious; unified and diverse; liturgical and open to the spontaneity of the Spirit; catholic and evangelical; and finally sacramental and missional. I don't believe that I am alone. Many have found in the historic Anglican tradition an oasis in the desert, a river in dry and thirsty land, and a treasure hidden among the clamor of our postmodern society. It is a great gift, and I want to encourage others to discover this beautiful tradition for themselves.

If you are looking for a vibrant expression of the Christian faith that is scriptural and deeply rooted in historic Christianity, come and see what millions of Christians around the world have found in Anglicanism. Pick up the Book of Common Prayer and begin to pray, continue studying the Anglican way, and most importantly, come and worship with us by visiting an Anglican church in your area.

GLOSSARY OF ANGLICAN TERMS

Absolution: A declaration by a bishop or priest, announcing forgiveness by God to those who have confessed their sins.

Acolyte: A lay volunteer who assists the priest in worship.

Alb: A full-length white vestment that was the basic liturgical garment of the early church.

Altar Guild: A group of lay people in a church who prepare the altar and maintain the furnishings in a church building.

Anglican: A term which comes from the word *angle*, "Anglican" actually means "English" and refers to the church's place of origin.

Apostolic Succession: The doctrine which holds that bishops are the direct successors of the original apostles in an unbroken line to the ministry to which Jesus Himself ordained the apostles.

Archbishop: A bishop in charge of a group of dioceses in a geographical area. The form of address is "The Most Reverend" or "Your Grace."

Archdeacon: A priest who is part of a bishop's staff and usually has administrative supervision over the diocese.

Baptism: The sacrament of baptism occurs when a candidate is immersed in or has water poured on him or her in the name of the Father, the Son, and the Holy Spirit. Baptism has multiple meanings, including cleansing from sin and being adopted by God into His family.

GLOSSARY

Bishop: A bishop is the chief pastor of a local diocese of churches. The bishop stands as the guardian of the faith, fosters unity, executes discipline when needed, and proclaims the Word of God. The title "bishop" comes from the New Testament Greek word *epískopos*, which means "overseer." Bishops wear purple shirts and a large gold cross.

Book of Common Prayer: A collection of historic prayers, devotions, and services that was originally compiled by Thomas Cranmer. Commonly called the "Prayer Book" and often abbreviated as the BCP.

Cassock: A black robe worn by priests or deacons, usually with a white over-garment called a surplice. Lay readers, choir members, and acolytes also wear cassocks.

Catechism: A historic form of discipleship that is usually based on questions and answers. The Greek word for "instruct" or "teach" is *katecheo*, from which we get our English word "catechize."

Cathedral: The church in which the diocesan bishop is seated and is often the gathering place for many of the diocese's major worship celebrations and events. The rector of a cathedral is given the title of Dean of the Cathedral.

Catholic: A term that is used in the historic creeds and literally means "universal."

Celebrant: The person who leads the worship service. In a Eucharist, the celebrant is the bishop, or someone whom the bishop appoints to lead the service for him or her.

Censer: A vessel in which incense is burned on charcoal.

GLOSSARY

Chalice: The cup that contains the wine used at Communion.

Chalice-bearer: The person who administers the chalice during Communion.

Chancel: The section of a church building between the nave and the sanctuary; usually the place where the choir sits.

Chasuble: An oval-shaped liturgical vestment worn by the celebrant during Communion.

Ciborium: A cup that resembles a chalice, except that it has a re-movable lid. A ciborium is used to hold communion wafers during the Eucharist.

Clergy: A group of ordained people who have been consecrated for ministry in the church.

Collect: A prayer that is designed to "collect" the thoughts of the lessons and bind the thoughts of the congregation together.

Confirmation: When a person makes a public confession and affir-mation of their faith, fulfilling the vows their godparents made for them at their baptism. The bishop lays his hands on them and prays for the Holy Spirit to strengthen them.

Consecration: The word literally means "to set aside" (for special divine use). At the Eucharist, the elements of bread and wine are consecrated during the liturgy.

Corporal: A square piece of linen that is laid on top of the altar cloth at Communion.

GLOSSARY

Crosier: The bishop's staff, which is carried in a procession and held when giving the absolution or blessing.

Cruet: A glass or metal vessel that is used to hold the water and wine for the Eucharist.

Daily Office: Another name for the historic pattern of prayer that includes Morning and Evening Prayer.

Deacon: A "servant" and the first order of ordained ministry. There are "transitional" deacons, who will eventually be ordained as priests, and "vocational" deacons, who will serve as deacons for the rest of their lives.

Diocese: A diocese is a cluster of churches in a distinct geographic region under the leadership of a bishop. The adjectival form of the term is diocesan.

Elements: The bread and wine of Holy Communion.

Episcopal: The name of a form of church organization, which means governed by a bishop.

Eucharist: Literally means "thanksgiving," and refers to the service of Holy Communion.

Father: A familiar title referring to a priest.

Font: A basin for water to be used in church baptisms.

Fraction: The part of the Communion liturgy where the celebrant breaks the Communion bread.

GLOSSARY

Holy Orders: The threefold order of ordained ministry, consisting of the offices of bishop, priest, and deacon, that emerged early in the life of the church and continues today.

Homily: Another name for a sermon.

Host: The consecrated "bread" of the Holy Communion.

Laity: The non-ordained members of a church, as distinguished from the clergy.

Lectionary: A list of Bible passages for personal reading and study, or for preaching in services of worship. The Lectionary readings from the Book of Common Prayer are used for daily services of worship and for Morning and Evening Prayer.

Liturgical: The word liturgy comes from the Greek word *leitourgia*, which means "the work of people." Today, the word "liturgy" generally refers to a set form of words, actions, and rituals done in worship.

Narthex: An enclosed space at the entry end of the nave of a building; the area in the church building inside the doors and in front of the nave.

Nave: The main part of a church building and the place where the congregation sits.

Oblation: The act of offering the Eucharistic gifts to God in the Communion service.

Offetory: Includes the offering of money, and of bread and wine that is to be consecrated during the Communion.

GLOSSARY

Paten: The vessel used to contain the consecrated bread during Communion.

Priest: Shares with the bishop in the overseeing of the church by serving as a pastor to the people. The priest proclaims the gospel and is authorized to administer the sacraments in the local church.

Primate: A title for archbishops of the Anglican Communion that distinguishes them from other bishops in the same province.

Province: A particular geographic grouping of dioceses usually representing a nation. The minimum to constitute a province is usually four dioceses. Some provinces have distinct boundaries of political states, while some include multiple nations.

Purificator A small piece of white linen used at Communion to cleanse the chalice by wiping its rim.

Sacraments: Outward and visible signs of inward and spiritual grace. Sacraments are signs and actions that point us to deeper realities than we are able to experience with our five senses.

Sanctus: The part of the Holy Communion service that begins with the words, "Holy, Holy, Holy."

Stole: A long, thin liturgical vestment worn only by the clergy. Bishops and priests wear it around the neck and the shoulder, and deacons wear it over the left shoulder.

Surplice: A white vestment often made of linen and worn over a cassock.

GLOSSARY

Unction: The process of anointing someone with oil for religious purposes. Anglicans also use the word to refer to anointing the sick.

Vestments: Clothing appropriate to persons (clergy and laity) participating in liturgical actions.

Vestry: A group of women and men who are elected by the congregation to handle the temporal, everyday affairs of the church.

Via Media: A Latin phrase that means "the middle way." The middle way allows us to synthesize great Christian truths into a central core, rather than focusing on extremes.

Vicar: An English term referring to a priest in charge of a mission. It is the typical title used today to describe an English priest in who is charge of a local congregation.

Wafer: A small, very thin, round piece of bread used in the Lord's Supper that is often unleavened. Sometimes the wafer is imprinted with a cross.

ENDNOTES

INTRODUCTION
1. This is not just an anecdotal observation but is based on ethnographic research I conducted a few years ago on young adults who are embracing liturgy in the United States. See Winfield Bevins, *Ever Ancient, Ever New: The Allure of Liturgy for a New Generation* (Grand Rapids, MI: Zondervan, 2019).
2. See Lesslie Newbigin, *The Household of God: Lectures on the Nature of the Church* (Eugene, OR: Wipf & Stock, 2008), 87.
3. Anglican Church in North America, *The Book of Common Prayer (2019)*, 484.
4. Rowan Williams, *Anglican Identities* (Cambridge, MA: Cowley Publications, 2003), 2.
5. See https://anglicancompass.com/.
6. Timothy Tennent, *Invitation to World Missions: A Trinitarian Missiology for the Twenty-first Century* (Grand Rapids, MI: Kregel, 2010), 31.
7. These come from the "Anglican journey" stories told at Anglican Compass, unless otherwise noted. See https://anglicancompass.com/tag/anglican-journey/.

CHAPTER ONE
1. Drew Haltom, "My Anglican Journey: Burnout and Hope," https://anglicancompass.com/my-anglican-journey-burnout-and-hope/.
2. See Edward L. Smither, *Missionary Monks: An Introduction to the History and Theology of Missionary Monasticism* (Eugene, OR: Cascade Books, 2016), 64–81.
3. Bede, *A History of the English Church and People* (London, England: Penguin Books, 1968), 73.
4. From Winfield Bevins, *Ever Ancient, Ever New*, 12.
5. Cited in John Foxe, *Foxe's Book of Martyrs* (New Kensington, PA: Whitaker House, 1981), 309–10.
6. John Foxe, *Foxe's Book of Martyrs*, 309.
7. Michael Ramsey, *The Anglican Spirit* (New York: Seabury Classics, 2004), 53.
8. It is worth noting that not everyone agrees with the reliability of the numerical growth of the Anglican Communion because the number of active Anglicans could be far lower. For instance, the figure of 80

million includes 26 million Anglicans in England, when there are in fact just under one million regular churchgoers. See David Goodhew, *Growth and Decline in the Anglican Communion 1980 to the Present.* (London: Routledge, 2017). See also Daniel Muñoz "North to South: A Reappraisal of Anglican Communion Membership Figures," *Journal of Anglican Studies* 14, no. 1 (2016): 71–95.
9. Phillip Jenkins, *The Next Christendom: The Coming of Global Christianity* (Oxford, Oxford University Press, 2002), 59.
10. If you are interested in reading the biographies of great Anglicans, see Richard H. Schmidt's *Glorious Companions: Five Centuries of Anglican Spirituality* (Grand Rapids, MI: Eerdmans, 2002).
11. *Lesser Feasts and Fasts 2006* (Church Publishing Incorporated, 2006), 265.

CHAPTER TWO
1. Emily McGowin, "A Gift of God," https://anglicancompass.com/a-gift-of-god-by-rev-dr-emily-mcgowin/.
2. C. S. Lewis, *Mere Christianity* (New York: Collier Books, 1952), vi.
3. Wesley Hill, The Living Church, May 18, 2015, http://livingchurch.org/covenant/2015/05/18/is-there-an-anglican-understanding-of-the-new-testament/.
4. *Historic Creeds and Confessions*, electronic ed. (Oak Harbor: Lexham Press, 1997).
5. Source: https://www.churchofengland.org/prayer-and-worship/worship-texts-and-resources/book-common-prayer/articles-religion.
6. Gerald Bray, *The Faith We Confess: An Exposition of the Thirty-Nine Articles* (London: The Latimer Trust, 2009).
7. J. C. Ryle, *Knots Untied* (first published in 1877). Cited in http://www.churchsociety.org/issues_new/doctrine/39a/iss_doctrine_39A_Ryle.asp.
8. http://anglicansonline.org/basics/Chicago_Lambeth.html.
9. J. I. Packer and Gary A. Parrett, "The Lost Art of Catechesis: It's a Tried and True Way of Teaching, among Other Things, Christian Doctrine," *Christianity Today*, March 12, 2010, http://www.christianitytoday.com/ct/2010/march/14.26.html.
10. J. I. Packer and Gary A. Parrett, "The Lost Art of Catechesis."
11. *To Be a Christian: An Anglican Catechism*, ed. J. I. Packer and Joel Scandrett (Wheaton, IL: Crossway, 2020). Available online at https://anglicanchurch.net/catechism/.
12. Michael Ramsey, *The Anglican Spirit*, 7.
13. "The Collect for Trinity Sunday," BCP 2019, 615.

ENDNOTES

CHAPTER THREE
1. Michael F. Bird, "Why Be Anglican? My Story." https://www.patheos.com/blogs/euangelion/2019/02/why-be-anglican/.
2. J. I. Packer, "The Anglican Commitment to Comprehensiveness: A Kind of Noah's Ark?" http://www.virtueonline.org/anglican-commitment-comprehensiveness-jipacker.
3. Cited by James Wood in "God Talk: The Book of Common Prayer at three hundred and fifty," *The New Yorker*, Oct. 22, 2012, http://www.newyorker.com/magazine/2012/10/22/god-talk.
4. Daniel Swift, "Shakespeare and the Book of Common Prayer," *HuffPost Religion*, Nov. 16, 2012, http://www.huffingtonpost.com/daniel-swift/shakespeare-and-the-book-of-common-prayer_b_1885211.html.
5. Cited in Winfield Bevins, *Our Common Prayer: A Field Guide to the Book of Common Prayer* (Charleston, SC: Simeon Press, 2003), 21.
6. Winfield Bevins, *Our Common Prayer*, iii.
7. Winfield Bevins, *Our Common Prayer*, 162.
8. Winfield Bevins, *Our Common Prayer*, 162.
9. Winfield Bevins, *Ever Ancient, Ever New*, 12.
10. "A Prayer of Self-Dedication" by William Temple, BCP 2019, 668.

CHAPTER FOUR
1. N.T. Wright, *After You Believe: Why Christian Character Matters*. (New York: HarperOne, 2010), 222.
2. John Wesley, *John Wesley's Sunday Service of the Methodists in North America* (Quarterly Review Reprint Series, 1984), A 1.
3. Jonathan Groves, "My Anglican Journey: A Sunday Service that Directs Me to Christ," https://anglicancompass.com/my-anglican-journey-a-sunday-service-that-directs-me-to-christ/.
4. Donald McKim, *Westminster Dictionary of Theological Terms* (Louisville, KY: Westminster John Knox Press, 1996), 163.
5. Frank C. Senn, *Introduction to Christian Liturgy* (Minneapolis: Fortress Press, 2012), 5.
6. The twofold structure of Word and Table can be found in Justin Martyr's *First Apology*, dating AD 150. See *The Nicene and Post-Nicene Fathers* (Grand Rapids: Eerdmans, 1960). According to James W. Farrell, "The liturgy as a whole is composed of two parts, "Word" and "Sacrament," and each of those parts has a central element within it." James W. Farrell, *The Liturgy Explained* (New York: Morehouse Publishing, 2013), 15. See also Gregory Dix, *The Shape of the Liturgy*

(London: Continuum, 1945).
7. James W. Farrell, *The Liturgy Explained*, 15–18.
8. BCP 2019, 130.
9. According to R.C.D. Jasper, "In the singular the word 'liturgy' denotes an act of worship, more specifically the eucharist." *The Westminster Dictionary of Worship*, 222. James W. Farrell also says, "The Liturgy is the shorthand term we use for the service of worship called by various families of Christian faith and practice, The Holy Eucharist…" *The Liturgy Explained*, 2.
10. G.A. Mitchell, *Westminster Dictionary of Worship*, 174.
11. See Oscar Cullmann, *Early Christian Worship* (London: SCM, 1953), 21. Many of the early Church Fathers spoke about the regularity of the Eucharist in the church's life and worship, including Cyprian, Ambrose, Basil, and Chrysostom, who wrote about the Eucharist as a daily practice in the life of the church. See also Burton Scott Easton, *The Apostolic Tradition of Hippolytus* (Hamden, Conn.: Archon, 1962), 33–36.
12. Esau McCaulley, "Black and Anglican: A Maundy Thursday Conversion Story," https://esaumccaulley.com/2019/04/18/black-and-anglican-a-maundy-thursday-conversion-story/.
13. N. T. Wright, "On Earth as in Heaven" a sermon at the Eucharist on the Sunday after Ascension Day, York Minster, 20 May 2007, http://ntwrightpage.com/sermons/Earth_Heaven.htm.
14. BCP 2019, 106.
15. BCP 1979, 833.

CHAPTER FIVE

1. *To Be a Christian: An Anglican Catechism* (Wheaton, IL: Crossway, 2020), 55, Q121.
2. Alexander Schmemann, *For the Life of the World: Sacraments and Orthodoxy* (Crestwood, NY: St. Vladimir's Seminary Press, 1963), 27.
3. Robert Webber and Lester Ruth, *Evangelicals on the Canterbury Trail: Why Evangelicals Are Attracted to the Liturgical Church* (New York, Morehouse Publishing, 1985), 47.
4. See Shawn McCain, "Introducing The Sacramental Imagination," https://anglicancompass.com/introducing-the-sacramental-imagination/.
5. *To Be a Christian: An Anglican Catechism*, 56, Q123.
6. *To Be a Christian: An Anglican Catechism*, 57, Q127.
7. Cited in David A. DeSilva, *Sacramental Life: Spiritual Formation*

ENDNOTES

Through the Book of Common Prayer (Downers Grove, IL: Intervarsity Press, 2008), 21.
8. *To Be a Christian: An Anglican Catechism*, 57, Q129.
9. John Stott, "The Evangelical Doctrine of Baptism," *Churchman* 112, no. 1 (1998): https://churchsociety.org/docs/churchman/112/Cman_112_1_Stott.pdf.
10. *To Be a Christian: An Anglican Catechism*, 58, Q132–33.
11. *To Be A Christian: An Anglican Catechism*, 58–59, Q134.
12. Many of the early Church Fathers spoke about the regularity of the Eucharist in the church's life and worship, including Cyprian, Ambrose, Basil, and Chrysostom, who wrote about the Eucharist as a daily practice in the life of the church.
13. Compare Acts 2:42–46 with Paul's use of the word *koinonia* in 1 Corinthians 11:20–34.
14. Luke Timothy Johnson includes this observation in his discussion on Jesus in the memory of the church. He says that, "*Anamnesis* in earliest Christianity was even more complex, for the one remembered from the past was also being experienced as present here and now," *The Writings of the New Testament* (Minneapolis, MN: Fortress Press, 1999), 125.
15. John Wesley, "The Duty of Constant Communion Sermon 101," *The Works of John Wesley*, Volume 2: Sermons 54–108.
16. Rowan Williams, *Being Christian: Baptism, Bible, Eucharist, Prayer* (Grand Rapids, MI: Eerdmans Publishing, 2014), 58.
17. *To Be a Christian: An Anglican Catechism*, 56, Q125.
18. Rowan Williams, *Being Christian*, 50.
19. "After Receiving Communion," BCP 2019, 676–77.

CHAPTER SIX
1. J. I. Packer and N.T Wright, *Anglican Evangelical Identity: Yesterday and Today* (London: The Latimer Trust, 2008), 18.
2. Article VI of the Sufficiency of the Holy Scripture for Salvation in the Book of Common Prayer, 868.
3. Thomas Cranmer, *Preface to the Great Bible*.
4. BCP 2019, 598.
5. John Howe, *Our Anglican Heritage* (Elgin, IL: David C. Cook, 1977), 23.
6. See http://www.pbs.org.uk/resources/bcp-350-supporters/.
7. Eugene Peterson, *Working the Angles: The Shape of Pastoral Integrity* (Grand Rapids, MI: Eerdmans, 1993), 50.
8. Thomas Cranmer, *Preface to the Great Bible*.

ENDNOTES

9. A.W. Tozer, *The Pursuit of God* (Camp Hill, PA. Christian Publications, 1993), 9.
10. "The Second Sunday in Advent," BCP 2019, 598.

CHAPTER SEVEN

1. Justin Clemente, "The Long Way Home: Dwelling in the Anglican Way," https://anglicancompass.com/the-long-way-home-dwelling-in-the-anglican-way-by-fr-justin-clemente/.
2. Ignatius, *Letter to the Magnesians* 2, 6:1.
3. "The Preface to the Ordinal," BCP 2019, 470.
4. Want to learn more about women's ordination debates within Anglicanism? Joshua Steele has put together some very helpful and informative resources at Anglican Compass. See https://anglicancompass.com/want-to-learn-more-about-womens-ordination-debates-within-anglicanism-start-with-these-resources/.
5. Source: The FAQ section at https://anglicanchurch.net/about/.
6. Article III. See https://anglicanchurch.net/wp-content/uploads/2020/02/CURRENT-C-and-C-2019.pdf.
7. BCP 1979, 871.
8. Phil Groves and Angharad Parry Jones, *Living Reconciliation*. (Cincinnati, Ohio: Forward Movement, 2014). xi.
9. The 2008 Global Anglican Future Conference (GAFCON) gathering brought together more than eleven hundred Anglican bishops, clergy, and laity from around the world. The goal of this gathering was not to break away from the Anglican Communion, but to unite orthodox Anglicans around the world. One of the outcomes of the GAFCON gathering was the formation of the Anglican Church in North America (ACNA) which was established in 2009. The unites 134,000 Anglicans in 1,062 congregations across the United States, Canada, and Mexico into a single Church.
10. There are numerous books and online articles about the challenges and divisions within the Anglican Communion from a variety of perspectives. I don't have the time or space in this chapter to do anything other than to acknowledge that it does exist. If you are interested, here are few places to start. See "A Statement by the Primates of the Anglican Communion meeting in Lambeth Palace October 15th and 16th, 2003." http://www.anglicannews.org/news/2003/10/a-statement-by-the-primates-of-the-anglican-communion-meeting-in-lambeth-palace.aspx. Ephraim Radner and Philip Turner, *The Fate of Communion: The Agony of Anglicanism and the Future of a Global*

ENDNOTES

Church. (Grand Rapids, MI: Wm. B. Eerdmans Publishing, 2006.) For a more recent book see also Gerald R. McDermott ed. *The Future of Orthodox Anglicanism* (Wheaton, IL: Crossway, 2020).
11. See Kevin Ward, A History of Global Anglicanism (Introduction to Religion) (Cambridge: Cambridge University Press, 2006).
12. Henry Luke Orombi, "What is Anglicanism?," *First Things* (August 2007): https://www.firstthings.com/article/2007/08/001-what-is-anglicanism.
13. "For the Human Family," BCP 2019, 659.

CHAPTER EIGHT
1. Timothy C. Tennent, "Homiletical Theology," Opening Convocation Address, Asbury Theological Seminary, September 2016. http://timothytennent.com/2016/09/13/my-2016-opening-convoca-tion-address-homiletical-theology/
2. Alvin L. Reid, *Radically Unchurched: Who They Are & How to Reach Them* (Grand Rapids, MI: Kregel Publications, 2002), 21.
3. George G. Hunter III, *The Recovery of a Contagious Methodist Movement* (Nashville, TN: Abingdon Press, 2011), 28.
4. Phil Zuckerman, *Living the Secular Life: New Answers to Old Questions* (New York: Penguin Books, 2015), 60.
5. Sunita Theiss, "My Anglican Journey," https://anglicancompass.com/my-anglican-journey-by-sunita-theiss/.
6. Bede, *The Ecclesiastical History of the English People* (Oxford: OUP, 2008). Stephen Neil also discusses the missionary expansion of the Anglican Church in *Anglicanism*. (Baltimore, MD: Penguin Books, 1958).
7. Bede, *Ecclesiastical History*, 144.
8. See Ray Simpson and Brent Lyons-Lee, *St. Aidan Way of Mission: Celtic Insights for a Post-Christian World* (Oxford: The Bible Reading Fellowship, 2016). See also Edward L. Smither, *Missionary Monks: An Introduction to the History and Theology of Missionary Monasticism* (Eugene, OR: Cascade Books, 2016), 64-81.
9. For a detailed discussion of England during Wesley's time period, see J. Wesley Bready, *England: Before and After Wesley* (New York: Russell & Russell, 1971).
10. See Winfield Bevins, *Marks of a Movement: What the Church Today Can Learn from the Wesleyan Revival* (Grand Rapids, MI: Zondervan, 2019). For more on Anglo-Catholic mission see Winfield Bevins, "Nothing New Under the Sun: 19th Century Church Planting in

ENDNOTES

England," https://livingchurch.org/2019/02/28/nothing-new-under-the-sun/; Winfield Bevins, "Real Presence: Reclaiming Anglo-Catholic Church Planting," https://anglicancompass.com/real-presence-reclaiming-the-legacy-of-anglo-catholic-church-planting/.

11. Drexel Gomez, "On Being Anglican in the Twenty-First Century," http://www.globalsouthanglican.org/comments/on_being_anglican_in_the_21st_century_abp_drexel_gomez/.
12. Lesslie Newbigin, *The Open Secret: An Introduction to the Theology of Mission* (Grand Rapids: Eerdmans, 1995), 18.
13. Lesslie Newbigin, "The Mission of the Triune God," (1962), 12. This is an unpublished paper that can be found online at the Newbigin Resources website: http://newbiginresources.org/1962-the-mission-of-the-triune-god/. The website is dedicated to the life and work of Bishop J. E. Lesslie Newbigin . It combines full text of many of his writings, searchable by title, and also includes many of his audio lectures and speeches.
14. Lesslie Newbigin, *The Open Secret*, 40.
15. Lesslie Newbigin, *The Open Secret*, 40.
16. Lesslie Newbigin, *The Open Secret*, 56.
17. Richard Chartres, "New Fire in London," Lambeth Lecture, September 30, 2015. http://www.archbishopofcanterbury.org/articles.php/5621/bishop-of-london-delivers-lambeth-lecture-on-church-growth-in-the-capital/.
18. For more on the Gregory Center for Church Multiplication, visit https://www.ccx.org.uk/about.
19. This is taken from an online interview Ric Thorpe gave to Asbury Seminary: https://asburyseminary.edu/voices/26615.
20. See https://alphausa.org/.
21. For more information, see https://alphausa.org/endorsements.
22. Travis Collins, *Fresh Expressions of Church* (Franklin, TN: Seedbed Publishing, 2015), 5.
23. See http://freshexpressions.org.uk/about/what-is-a-fresh-expression/.
24. Archbishop's Council on Mission and Public Affairs, *Mission-Shaped Church: Church Planting and Fresh Expressions in a Changing Context* (New York: Seabury Books, 2009), 26.
25. The Church of England, "The Declaration of Assent." Available online at https://www.churchofengland.org/prayer-and-worship/worship-texts-and-resources/common-worship/ministry/declaration-assent/.
26. Archbishop's Council on Mission and Public Affairs, *Mission-Shaped Church*, 34.

ENDNOTES

27. Church Army's Research Unit, "The Day of Small Things: An Analysis of Fresh Expressions of Church in
28. 21 Dioceses of the Church of England," (November 2016), 10. Available online at https://www.churcharmy.org/.
29. Church Army's Research Unit, "The Day of Small Things," 10.
30. Greenough White, *An Apostle of the Western Church Memoir of the Right Reverend Jackson Kemper Doctor of Divinity, First Missionary Bishop of the American Church With Notices of Some of His Contemporaries.*(New York: Thomas Whittaker, 1900).
31. See Theodore I. Holcombe, B.D., *An Apostle of the Wilderness: James Lloyd Breck, D.D. His Missions and His Schools* (New York: Thomas Whittaker, 1903). To understand his missionary legacy, also visit Nashotah House Seminary website at https://www.nashotah.edu/.
32. Todd Hunter, *The Accidental Anglican: The Surprising Appeal of the Liturgical Church* (Downers Grove, IL: InterVarsity Press, 2010), 115.
33. See the website for Anglican Multi-Ethnic Network. https://anglican-multiethnic.org.
34. Amber Noel, "Anglicanism and the Black Future: An Interview." *The Living Church*, May 15, 2020. https://livingchurch.org/covenant/2020/05/15/anglicanism-and-the-black-future-an-interview/.
35. See the US Census report: https://www.census.gov/newsroom/press-releases/2018/cb18-41-population-projections.html.
36. George G. Hunter III, *The Recovery of a Contagious Methodist Movement*, 28.
37. Martin Robinson, *Planting Mission-Shaped Churches Today* (Oxford, UK: Monarch Books, 2006), 144.
38. See http://www.anglicancommunion.org/mission/marks-of-mission.aspx.
39. Emil Brunner, *The Word and the World* (London: Student Christian Movement Press, 1931), 108.
40. "For the Mission of the Church," BCP 2019, 651.

CHAPTER NINE

1. See H. D. Weidner, *The Via Media of the Anglican Church by John Henry Newman* (Oxford: Clarendon Press, 1990).
2. See Howard Snyder, *The Radical Wesley: The Patterns and Practices of a Movement Maker* (Franklin, TN: Seedbed, 2014).
3. Alister McGrath, "The Tradition Continues," *Christian History Magazine,* Issue 48 (vol. xiv, no. 4), 40.
4. Alister McGrath, *The Renewal of Anglicanism*, (London: SPCK, 1993), 129.
5. From a speech at a meeting marking his return from a tour of Australia and New Zealand, Westminster Central Hall, 30 Jan. 1951,

ENDNOTES

(*Church Times*, 2 Feb. 1951), 1.
6. Michael Ramsey, *The Gospel and the Catholic Church: Recapturing a Biblical Understanding of the Church as the Body of Christ* (Peabody, MA: Hendrickson Publishers, 2009), 178–79.
7. J. I. Packer cited in Roger Steer, *Guarding the Holy Fire: The Evangelicalism of John R. W. Stott, J. I. Packer, and Alister McGrath* (Grand Rapids, MI: Baker Books, 1999), 218.
8. Glenn Packiam, "Why I'm Becoming an Anglican Priest at New Life Church," https://churchleaders.com/worship/worship-blogs/173300-why-i-m-becoming-an-anglican-priest-at-new-life-church.html.
9. Paul F. M. Zahl, *The Protestant Face of Anglicanism* (Grand Rapids, MI: Wm. B. Eerdmans, 1998), 71.
10. Elizabeth Peterson, "Can I Watch You Pray?" https://anglicancompass.com/anglican-journeys-elizabeth-peterson/.
11. For a thought-provoking article on the influence of the Charismatic within Anglicanism, see Dale M. Coulter's "A Charismatic Invasion of Anglicanism?" in *First Things*: http://www.firstthings.com/blogs/firstthoughts/2014/01/neither-an-invasion-nor-surprising-lambeth-palace-chemin-neuf-and-anglican-charismatics.
12. See Trinity Anglican Mission website at http://atltrinity.org/beliefs-and-practices/.
13. http://www.truroanglican.com/wp-content/uploads/Tract_The-Anglican-Tradition.pdf
14. Richard Schmidt, *Glorious Companions: Five Centuries of Anglican Spirituality*, xxi.
15. John Stott, *The Living Church: Convictions of a Lifelong Pastor* (Downers Grove, IL: IVP Books, 2007), 161.
16. This quote is taken Fleming Rutledge's personal website: https://generousorthodoxy.org. Generous Orthodoxy is a term that originally comes from Hans Frei, a theologian at Yale Divinity School in the 1970s and 80s.
17. Cited in Howard Chandler Robbins, "The Panama Congress and the Protestant Episcopal Church," *The Missionary Review of the World* 29 (New Series; Vol. 39, Old Series; 1916), 21.
18. "For the Unity of the Church," BCP 1979, 818.

CONCLUSION
1. Cited in Leland Ryken, *J. I. Packer: An Evangelical Life* (Wheaton, IL: Crossway, 2015).

ANGLICAN ⊕ COMPASS
Your Guide to Anglican Life

*We help you
navigate the Anglican tradition
with clarity & charity.*

Learn more at
anglicancompass.com

Made in the USA
Coppell, TX
31 January 2022

72764733R00100